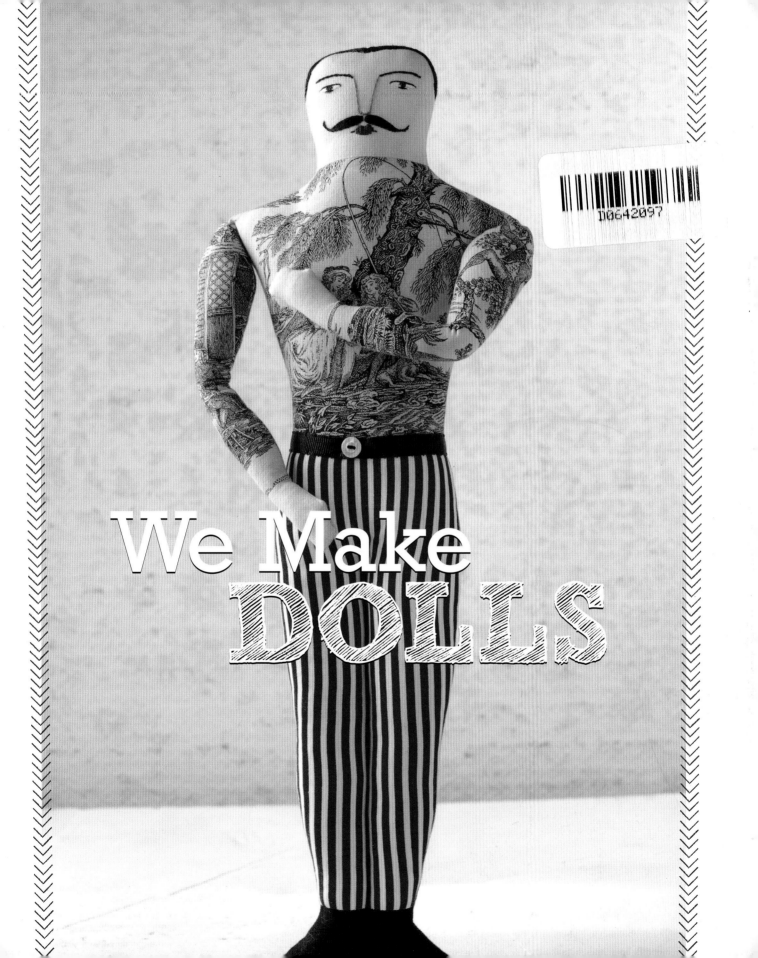

We Make DOLLS

We Make

DOLLS

Top Dollmakers Share Their Secrets & Patterns

Jenny Doh

LARK CRAFTS
Asheville

Editor: Jenny Doh

Writer: B. Glass

Copyeditor: Jane LaFerla

Assistant Editors: Gail Ellspermann, Nancy D. Wood, Jana Holstein

Designer: Nadine Alvillar

Project Photographer: Cynthia Shaffer

Cover Designer: Kristi Pfeffer

LARK CRAFTS

An Imprint of Sterling Publishing
387 Park Avenue South
New York, NY 10016

If you have questions or comments about
this book, please visit: larkcrafts.com

Library of Congress Cataloging-in-Publication Data

Doh, Jenny.
  We make dolls! : top dollmakers share their secrets & patterns / Jenny Doh. -- 1st ed.
      p. cm.
  Includes index.
  ISBN 978-1-4547-0249-8 (pb-trade pbk. : alk. paper)
  1. Dollmaking. I. Title.
  TT175.D567 2012
  745.592--dc23

                                        2011036220
10 9 8 7 6 5 4 3 2 1

First Edition

Published by Lark Crafts
An Imprint of Sterling Publishing Co., Inc.
387 Park Avenue South, New York, NY 10016

Text © 2012, Jenny Doh
Photography © 2012, Lark Crafts, an Imprint of Sterling Publishing Co., Inc., unless otherwise specified
Illustrations © 2012, Lark Crafts, an Imprint of Sterling Publishing Co., Inc., unless otherwise specified

Distributed in Canada by Sterling Publishing,
c/o Canadian Manda Group, 165 Dufferin Street
Toronto, Ontario, Canada M6K 3H6

Distributed in the United Kingdom by GMC Distribution Services,
Castle Place, 166 High Street, Lewes, East Sussex, England BN7 1XU

Distributed in Australia by Capricorn Link (Australia) Pty Ltd.,
P.O. Box 704, Windsor, NSW 2756 Australia

Manufactured in China

ISBN 13: 978-1-4547-0249-8

For information about custom editions, special sales, and premium and corporate purchases, please contact Sterling Special Sales Department at 800-805-5489 or specialsales@sterlingpub.com.

Requests for information about desk and examination copies available to college and university professors must be submitted to academic@larkbooks.com. Our complete policy can be found at www.larkcrafts.com.

Table of Contents

Getting Started

The majority of the projects in this book are soft dolls. In this section, you'll find valuable information you can use for making these adorable stitched creations. The book also contains three needle-felted dolls created by Jenn Docherty. You will find specific information for the needle-felting technique on page 103. As you work on the projects, you may find some unfamiliar names of tools, materials, or techniques. If you do, refer to the Glossary on page 159, which should help clear up any questions.

Before You Begin

As you start diving into these projects, you will soon discover the joy of doll making. Once you select the doll that you'd like to create, the first thing you will want to do is gather all the tools and materials listed for that doll. The how-to photos, along with those of the finished dolls, are presented to work hand-in-hand with the project instructions. Provided below is important information about templates and seam allowances that will help you with the overall process.

Templates

Each project has a Before You Begin section where the artist gives directions for using her templates. The pattern templates for the projects are found toward the back of the book. Most templates are the exact size you need. Others need to be enlarged at a copy center on machines that can enlarge per the specified percentages listed. Once you've sized the templates, you can cut them out and use them to start cutting your fabrics.

As you cut the fabric pieces, be sure to transfer all markings from the templates, including notches for darts and openings for turning and stuffing. Pay close attention to the number of cuts for each template piece, along with specific instructions for reversing the template for some cuts. For example, to create two arms, you'll sometimes need to make four cuts of the arm template, with two of the cuts reversed (a mirror image of the other two arms).

DOLL MAKING TOOL KIT

Assembling a basic tool kit ensures that you'll have everything at hand when you're ready to get to work. The list below contains the basic materials and tools needed to create the stitched soft dolls in this book. Each individual project will also list the fabrics and any additional tools and materials that are unique to creating that specific doll.

* Sewing machine
* Scissors
* Pinking shears
* Pencil
* Measuring tape and ruler
* Straight pins
* Safety pins
* Fabric spray adhesive
* Paper-backed fusible web
* Iron and pressing cloth

* Water-soluble fabric marker
* Polyester fiberfill
* Hand sewing needles
* Embroidery needles
* Chopstick, knitting needle, or other thin, pointy utensil for turning
* 5-inch (12.7 cm) doll needle

Seam Allowances

Information about seam allowances is also found in the Before You Begin section for each project—be mindful of these instructions since they vary from artist to artist.

Several of the dollmakers provide templates with seam allowances already built in. For those projects, you'll trace the shapes onto the wrong side of the fabric, cut them out, and sew according to the seam allowances specified in the project instructions.

There are other artists who provide templates without seam allowances. In those instances, you will trace the shapes onto the wrong side of the fabric and cut the fabric larger than the template piece by ¼ inch (6 mm) or by another specified seam allowance.

EMBROIDERY AND HAND STITCHES

These are the most common hand and embroidery stitches you'll need for making the dolls in this book. Use them when closing an opening, stitching around an appliqué, or embroidering facial features.

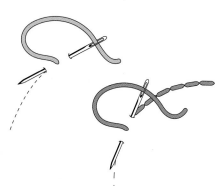

Backstitch
Use the backstitch for holding seams together under pressure. You can also use it to outline shapes.

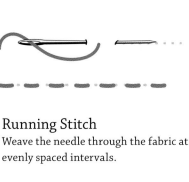

French Knot
Perfect for making eyes, or whenever you want to add interest or texture.

Slipstitch
This stitch is perfect for closing the openings. Anchor the thread by slipping the needle through one end of the open seam, take a small stitch through the fold, and then pull the needle through. In the other side of the seam, insert the needle directly opposite the stitch you just made, and take a stitch through the fold. Repeat.

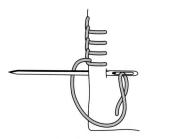

Blanket Stitch
Use this simple stitch to accentuate an edge.

Running Stitch
Weave the needle through the fabric at evenly spaced intervals.

Satin Stitch
Make parallel rows of straight stitches to fill in an outline.

Chain Stitch
This stitch will follow a line or make a flower when stitched in a circle.

Ladder Stitch or Blind Stitch
Since you hide most of the thread in the folds, the ladder stitch is almost invisible when used to close an opening.

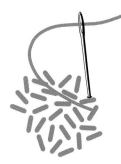

Seed Stitch
Make small straight stitches of the same length (and facing the same direction to fill in a shape with texture and color).

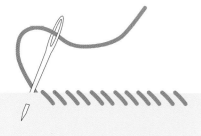

Overcast Stitch or Whipstitch

Sew the stitches over the edge of the fabrics when closing, or to bind the edges to prevent raveling.

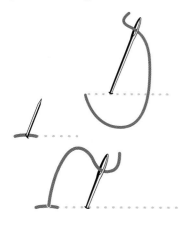

Split Stitch

Make a first stitch. Bring the needle up through the middle of the first stitch, splitting it. Continue with the needle coming up through the working thread to split the previous stitch.

Stem Stitch

Also known as the crewel stitch, use it to outline a shape.

Tips and Techniques

Being mindful of these valuable tips and techniques will help save time and ensure doll making success.

Clipping and Notching Curves

Once you've sewn the fabric pieces together, and before they are turned right side out, you'll need to clip or notch the curves to ensure smooth seams on the doll without puckering. You notch convex curves (or the hills), and clip concave curves (or the valleys). To notch, cut small V-shaped wedges from the seam allowance along the curve. To clip, make small snips in the seam allowance around the curve.

Turning and Stuffing

After clipping or notching all of the curves, turn the piece right side out. Polyester fiberfill is what most of the designers in this book use to stuff their dolls. The amount of stuffing is determined by the look the artist desires. Certain dolls will need to be firmly stuffed, while others are moderately stuffed.

Notch Convex Curves

Clip Concave Curves

The turning and stuffing process can be tricky, which is why having a chopstick or other long, pointy utensil on hand is recommended. Use it to help when you're turning narrow pieces, pushing out sharp curves, or getting the stuffing into tight spaces.

Raw-Edge Appliqué

Several dolls use raw-edge appliqués. This method is very easy—just cut and sew the appliqués without worrying about hemming the edges first. One of the simplest ways to attach the appliqués is to use paper-backed fusible web. First adhere a piece of fusible web to the wrong side of fabric, then lay the appliqué template on it, trace around the shape, and cut it out. Next, remove the paper backing, and then adhere the shape to the base fabric. Once in place, you can sew fairly close to the edges around the appliqué for added polish.

Rotating Joints

Some dolls are made with the arms and legs stitched into the seams or whipstitched onto the dolls: these lay flat with limited range of motion. For arms and legs that move freely, the trick is to attach the arms on a single cord (string, strong thread, or embroidery floss) that acts as a pivot. Another way is to secure a button on the outside of the first arm (without sewing it to the body), running the needle and thread straight through the doll body from shoulder to shoulder, then sewing the button to the opposite arm. Different dollmakers use slightly different techniques (a knot instead of a button, or a button with one hole), but the principle is the same.

Nichol BRINKMAN

www.pinkcheeksstudio.blogspot.com

Nichol Brinkman began sewing to release nervous energy when her mom was ill. What evolved were square and rectangular pillow monsters with button eyes and odd noses. Eventually these creatures morphed into more monster-shaped forms. As Nichol kept crafting, the monsters turned into people-type dolls. Her dolls today, which can be found in her popular Etsy shop, tend to come in bright colors and strong geometric shapes.

The Sharing Part of Art

It was after her mother's passing that she threw herself into doll making. When she first started, Nichol would wake up at unseemly hours if she had an idea and just start sewing. "We lived in a duplex then with thin walls, and I know I must have woken our neighbor with the sound of the machine." In fact, Nichol began sewing so much that she gave herself a repetitive stress injury and had to wear elbow pads.

All the time she had spent studying, critiquing, and composing art in college played a part in how Nichol designed her toys. Blogging became her main outlet for show and tell—the sharing part of art. "I started a blog and forced myself to sew a pillow monster each day for 30 days, and it was then that I started to feel like I belonged to a creative community again for the first time since art school. I loved it, and I continued sewing daily, well past the initial 30-day challenge."

From then on, Nichol's art has merged into Pink Cheeks Studio—a rather cheeky name for her blog and Etsy endeavors. "When I sold my first doll on Etsy and got some nice feedback about how much the buyer's son loved his new plushie, my world exploded!"

Stories through Observation

Her dolls evolved into beings with their own stories to tell. "I write bios for every doll I make. After I write their story, sometimes I need to add things to the doll, like a flower on the lapel or a plush hot-dog accessory." Not only do these minute details make her dolls more endearing and original, Nichol believes that the practice of writing these bios keeps her more observant.

She admits to borrowing unique quirks from the people in her life and weaving them into her dolls' stories. An example of this is Nichol's brother-in-law, "who is macho in many ways except for the drinks he orders. He always gets the most frilly, whipped-up, sprinkled-upon drink on the menu, so I borrowed that and turned it into someone's story."

EXPERT TIP
Drawing out design ideas in a sketch book is a great way to map out plans for new dolls, and to experiment with pen and paper how much to exaggerate facial features and body parts.

MR. STRONG

When you require heavy lifting, Mr. Strong leads the way. His colorful, appliquéd unitard prevents embarrassing wardrobe malfunctions.

WHAT YOU'LL NEED

* Templates (pages 123–125)
* Doll Making Tool Kit (page 7)
* Striped fabric, 2 pieces, each 6 x 7 inches (15.2 x 17.8 cm)
* Flesh-tone fabric, ½ yard (45.7 cm)
* White felt, 8 x 10 inches (20.3 x 25.4 cm)
* Red print fabric, 3 x 4 inches (7.62 x 10.16 cm)
* Red felt, 3 x 4 inches (7.6 x 10.2 cm)
* Pink felt, 4 x 4 inches (10.2 x 10.2 cm)
* Black felt, 6 x 6 inches (15.2 x 15.2 cm)
* Paper-backed fusible web, 2 pieces, each 6 x 7 inches (15.2 x 17.8 cm)
* Embroidery floss in black and pink
* 2 white buttons

FINISHED SIZE

* 7½ inches (19 cm) tall

Before You Begin

Cut out all template pieces along the solid cut lines. Templates without dotted lines do not have seam allowances and are cut as is. For a template with dotted sewing lines, first place the cut template on the wrong side of the corresponding fabric and trace. Remove the template and cut it down to the dotted lines. Place the template back on the corresponding fabric on the wrong side, and trace around it with a water-soluble fabric marker to mark the sewing line. Trace firmly so that the lines can be visible from the reverse side when sewing the body and the arms.

Fuse the paper-backed fusible web to the wrong sides of the striped fabric. Trace the unitard template on the paper backing, and cut the pieces out to make the appliqués. Set aside.

MAKING FACES

Making faces is a crucial part of the process. The entire personality of a doll can change just by moving the eyes a centimeter up or down, even if the eyes are just a simple embroidered French knot. In order to get the perfect face, Nichol's tip is to keep it simple and sketch it out until you feel the personality is just right.

What You Do

1 Place the body front right side up on upper body backing, aligning the curved top edges. On the outer edge only, stitch together ⅛ inch (3 mm) from the edge. Place body front and body back (right sides up) on an ironing surface. Remove paper backing from the unitard appliqués. Fuse one appliqué to the body front, and the other to the body back ⒜. Satin stitch the unitard neckline, and then straight stitch all remaining edges ⒝.

2 Place the fabric pieces for the nose and ears right sides together on their respective felt backings. Stitch and trim close to the seams. Notch the curves, then turn all pieces right side out and press on low heat.

3 Machine stitch the nose to the face ⒞. Hand sew the eyebrows and sideburns to the face with black embroidery floss using a running stitch or overcast stitch ⒟. Use overcast stitch with pink floss to attach the cheeks. Sew on the button eyes ⒠. Embroider the lines underneath the eyes with black floss. Place the beard on top of the teeth, and then place the assemblage on the face and pin. At the beard's edge closest to the teeth, begin machine stitching around the beard in ever increasing circles until you reach the outer edge ⒡. Embroider the lines of the teeth using black floss ⒢. Stitch the hair piece on the back.

4 Pin the ears to the front with their pink sides over the sideburns ⒣. Pin the body pieces with the right sides together, stitch, and then turn. Stuff the doll firmly with polyester fiberfill and hand sew the opening with a ladder stitch.

5 With right sides together, pin and then sew the arms. Notch the curves and carefully turn them right side out. Stuff each arm firmly with polyester fiberfill. Fold under the raw edge ½ inch (1.3 cm) to make a clean edge, and then ladder stitch both arms to the body ⒤. Use a damp cloth to remove any marks left by the water-soluble marker.

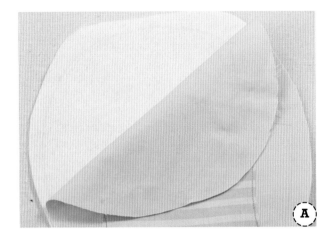

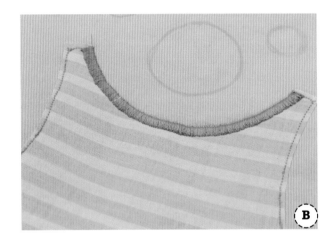

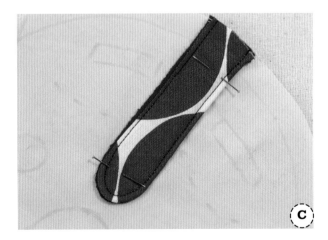

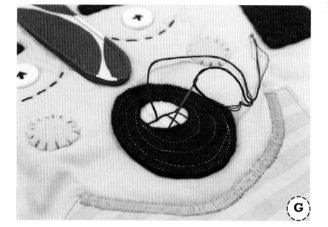

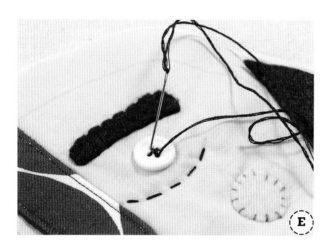

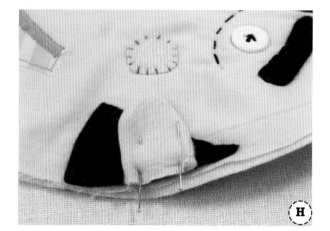

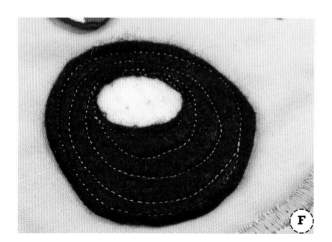

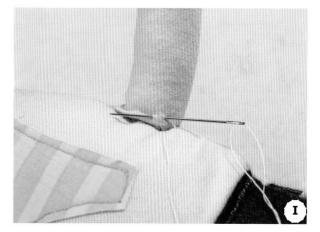

MR. GRUMPY IN A FROG SUIT

Honestly, would you be this grumpy if you were wearing such a cute outfit?

WHAT YOU'LL NEED

- ✳ Templates (pages 126–127)
- ✳ Doll Making Tool Kit (page 7)
- ✳ Scrap of striped fabric
- ✳ Scrap of paper-backed fusible web
- ✳ Flesh-tone fabric, 5 x 6 inches (12.7 x 15.2 cm)
- ✳ White felt, one 5-inch (12.7 cm) square
- ✳ Brown felt, one 5-inch (12.7 cm) square
- ✳ Scrap of pink felt
- ✳ Green wool felt, two 10-inch (20.4 cm) squares
- ✳ Denim, 2 pieces, each 4 x 7 inches (10.2 x 17.8 cm)
- ✳ Print fabric, 1 piece, 2 x 6 inches (5.1 x 15.2 cm)
- ✳ Embroidery floss in black and pink
- ✳ Dark red thread
- ✳ 2 White Buttons
- ✳ 1 Yellow Button

FINISHED SIZE

- ✳ 7 ½ inches (19 cm) tall

Before You Begin

Cut out all template pieces along the solid lines. Templates without dotted lines do not have seam allowances and are cut as is. For a template with dotted sewing lines, first place the cut template on the wrong side of the corresponding fabric and trace. Remove the template and cut it down to the dotted lines. Place the template back on the corresponding fabric on the wrong side, and trace around it with a water-soluble fabric marker to mark the sewing line. Press fusible web to the wrong side of the striped fabric before cutting out the nose. Do not cut arms until step 7.

What You Do

1 Lay the flesh-tone circle right side up over the white felt circle with edges aligned and stitch together. Peel the paper backing off the nose appliqué and fuse it to the face, then straight stitch around the nose, close to the edges (A). Pin the hair piece in place and stitch. Stitch a few lines into the felt to indicate hair. Position, then stitch the mustache into place. Use black embroidery floss and an overcast stitch to attach it to the face. Attach the cheeks using pink floss and the overcast stitch. Make the eyes with French knots using black floss (B).

2 Trim the face close to the stitching line around the circle. Pin the face on the felt front body piece. Straight stitch close to the face edge to secure. Using red thread, satin stitch over the straight stitching, going around the entire face (C).

3 Pin denim pants to a green body along the straight edges and stitch. Repeat for remaining pant and body (D). Press the seams open. Pin the front and back with right sides together. Stitch on the seam line, and leave an opening for turning (E).

4 Clip and notch curves and turn the body right side out. Stuff firmly with polyester fiberfill and ladder stitch the opening closed.

5 Sew the frog eye pieces together. Trim the seams, notch the curves, and turn right side out (**F**).

6 Fold edges in to make a clean edge. Stuff the eyes with polyester fiberfill and ladder stitch them to the top of the head (**G**).

7 Pin the two printed fabrics with right sides together, and stitch along one long edge. Press the seam to one side. Fold the stitched fabric in half with the seam running horizontally. Trace the arm template twice, leaving space for a seam allowance on all sides of both tracings. Stitch on the traced lines, leaving the short straight end open (**H**). Cut out the arms ¼ inch (6 mm) outside the seams. Clip the curves and turn right side out. Stuff the arms with polyester fiberfill, fold any excess fabric to make a clean edge, and whipstitch together. Sew the arms on to the doll (**I**).

8 Sew two white buttons to make the frog eyes, and add a yellow button below the face (**J**). Use a damp cloth to remove any marks left by the water-soluble marker.

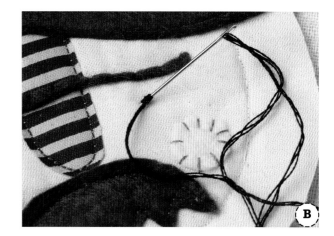

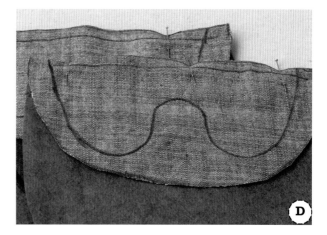

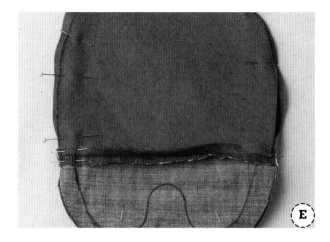

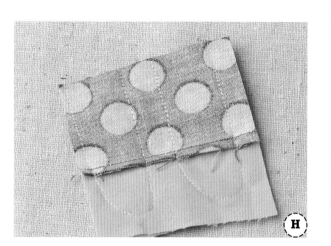

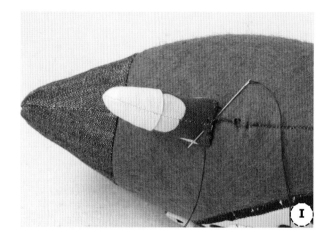

SUPER GIRL

She's not afraid. She's Super Girl!

WHAT YOU'LL NEED

* Templates (pages 128–130)
* Doll Making Tool Kit (page 7)
* Flesh-tone fabric, 7 x 4 inches (17.8 x 10.2 cm)
* White felt, 7 x 4 inches (17.8 x 10.2 cm)
* Red wool-blend felt, 8 x 12 inches (20.3 x 30.5 cm)
* Black felt, 1 x 5 inches (2.5 x 12.7 cm)
* Scrap of pink felt
* Scrap of red felt
* Print fabric, 8 x 12 inches (20.3 x 30.5 cm)
* Contrasting print fabric, 2 x 6 inches (5.1 x 15.2 cm)
* Faux fur, 3 x 12 inches (7.6 x 30.5 cm)
* Denim, 4 x 8 inches (10.2 x 20.3 cm)
* Metallic sewing-machine thread
* Embroidery floss in black and pink

FINISHED SIZE

* 18 inches (45.7 cm) tall

Before You Begin

Cut out all template pieces along the solid lines. Templates without dotted lines do not have seam allowances and are cut as is. For a template with dotted sewing lines, first place the cut template on the wrong side of the corresponding fabric and trace. Remove the template and cut it down to the dotted lines. Place the template back on the corresponding fabric on the wrong side, and trace around it with a water-soluble fabric marker to mark the sewing line.

What You Do

1 Lay the face right side up on the white felt with edges aligned and stitch (**A**). Lay one of the hair pieces on top of the face piece, then topstitch the felt around the face to attach (**B**).

2 Machine stitch the mask on the face using metallic thread, adding decorative stitches around the eyes as desired. Embroider dashed lines to create the eyebrows and nose, using a handsewing needle and two strands of black embroidery floss. Make the eyes with French knots, using two strands of black embroidery floss (**C**). Attach the cheeks using an overcast stitch and two strands of pink embroidery floss. Attach the lips with two strands of black embroidery floss.

3 Fold under both long edges of the decorative strip ½ inch (1.3 cm) and press. Center it on the front dress piece, pin, and then stitch (**D**). With right sides together, align the bottom edge of the face piece to the top edge of the front dress piece (**E**). Pin and stitch. Repeat for the back hair and dress pieces.

4 With right sides together, align the narrow edge of a faux-fur boot piece with a denim leg piece, pin, and sew. Repeat for all leg pieces. With right sides together, pin the pieces together, and stitch (**F**). Notch the curves and turn right side out. Stuff the legs with polyester fiberfill, leaving the top edge open.

5 Place the front of the doll on the back with right sides together and edges aligned. Place the legs in between with the toes pointing toward the head. Pin and stitch (G). Trim the seam allowances, notch the curves, and turn right side out. Firmly stuff with polyester fiberfill. Use a knitting needle or chopstick to help push the stuffing into the hair and all corners. Hand-sew the opening using the ladder stitch (H).

6 With right sides together, align the hand and arm pieces on the straight edges and stitch. Repeat for all arm pieces. With right sides together, pin the two hand/arm pieces, sew, and leave an opening for turning. Trim the seam allowances, notch the curves, and turn the piece right side out. Stuff the arms with polyester fiberfill, and hand sew the opening with a ladder stitch. Using a doll needle and two strands of embroidery floss, sew on one arm, then pass the needle and floss through the body to sew on the other arm (I). Make sure the floss is taut. Sew each arm twice to secure it to the body, passing the floss back through the body as needed before knotting off. Use a damp cloth to remove any marks left by the water-soluble marker.

STUFFY UNCLES

Nichol once had an uncle jokingly tell her to "grow up" when she told him at a family function that she sewed dolls. But that reaction was quite all right with Nichol. "I like to think that if you aren't doing something in your life that has your stuffy uncles scratching their heads, then maybe something needs to change!"

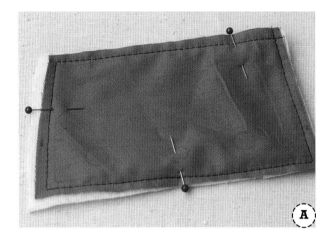

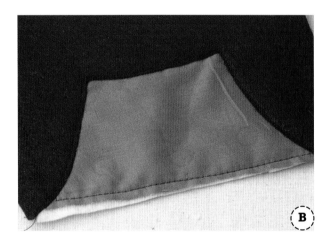

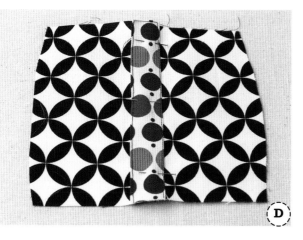

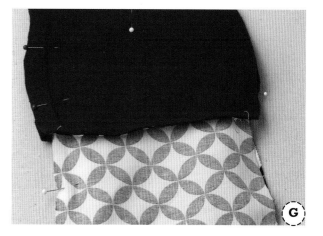

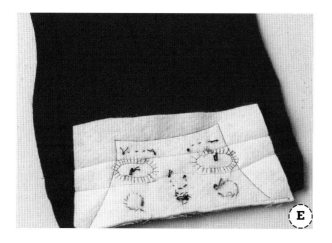

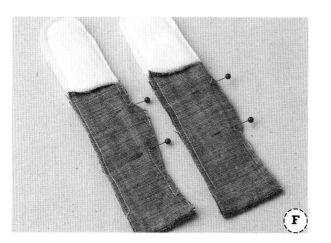

DANITA
www.danitaart.blogspot.com

If you're familiar with Danita's work, you know she dabbles in many mediums, including mixed-media and jewelry. You probably even know her for her vibrant use of color—you can see her colorful cast of characters in her Etsy shop. "I've noticed many of my pieces have red, black, green, and turquoise in them, but I try to force myself to use other combinations." To broaden her palette, she clips images from magazines for inspiration.

Danita Style

Books, videos, Internet research, and trial and error have made Danita the dollmaker she is today. "Everything comes with information and practice," she says. Her process is simple. Once she decides she's going to do something, she studies it, and then keeps trying to make it until she succeeds. "One of the wonders of the Internet is that you don't have to know someone who knows how to do something. You can research online, watch videos, or ask other people in forums and learn from that."

Danita is never without a challenge. She wants to learn how to sew clothing for herself and her children, as well as how to learn to make ceramics, musing about the day when she'll have free time. Her plan is to get a kiln, supplies, and just go for it—in true Danita style.

Taking Care of Others

Dolls began shaping Danita's life when she was very young. Danita's mother still cares for a little panda Danita made out of clay when she was three or four years old. "Dolls have been my imaginary friends," says Danita. "I enjoyed playing with them and telling them my secrets." Danita grew up with a variety of dolls made from different materials: rag, paper, plush, and plastic. Danita's grandmother would give her fabric scraps so she could make clothes for her dolls.

Her fondest memories include combing her dolls' hair and changing their clothes. Danita believes these acts are "natural things women do; taking care of others." Today, Danita focuses on being a mother and an artist, a job that entails taking care of others, including her dolls.

Studio Space in a Family Place

Danita designed her studio space for tending to work and family. With the addition of a third bedroom, her studio became the largest room in the house. There's even a space for her daughter to play with her own artsy stuff. Desks, bookshelves, and tables for jewelry making are all staples, but Danita believes her in-studio sink is one of the best things in the room! Her sewing machine and current projects sit on a table at the center, the heart of the room.

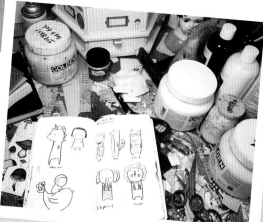

Before the birth of her son, Danita would work in the mornings while her daughter was at school and at night after her daughter went to sleep. Now Danita tries to work as efficiently as possible at night. "I decide what I'm doing that night, gather my supplies, and start working!" There's always music in the background. Danita's ever-growing iTunes library is currently at 13,700 songs, so you never know what will be playing.

EXPERT TIP

Free-motion stitching is a fun and easy way to add facial features to the dolls. You just need a darning foot and the ability to lower the feed dogs on your sewing machine. It takes a little bit of practice but once you get the hang of it, you will be able stitch eyes, nose, mouth, hairline, and other details in no time.

MERRY MERMAID

This sprightly mermaid loves her home under the sea, but she'll come out to play whenever you're around.

WHAT YOU'LL NEED

- ✳ Templates (pages 131–132)
- ✳ Doll Making Tool Kit (page 7)
- ✳ Muslin, 2 pieces, each 8 x 10 inches (20.3 x 25.4 cm), and 4 pieces, each 2 x 6 inches (5.1 x 15.2 cm)
- ✳ Yellow print fabric, 2 pieces, each 8 x 7 inches (20.3 x 17.8 cm)
- ✳ Blue print fabric, 2 pieces, each 12 x 12 inches (30.5 x 30.5 cm)
- ✳ 2 star appliqués
- ✳ Darning foot
- ✳ 2 buttons
- ✳ Strong thread or embroidery floss
- ✳ Cotton swab
- ✳ Pink chalk
- ✳ Organza ribbon

FINISHED SIZE

- ✳ 13 inches (33 cm) tall

Before You Begin

Cut out the templates along the solid lines. Lay the face/upper body template on one of the larger pieces of muslin, trace around it, and set aside. Cut all other pieces of fabric by adding a ¼-inch (6 mm) seam allowance around each shape. Transfer all markings to the wrong side of the fabric.

What You Do

1 Using the hairline and facial features on the template as a guide, mark these features on the uncut muslin template using a water-soluble fabric marker. Thread your sewing machine with black thread, attach the darning foot, and lower the feed dogs. Use free-motion sewing to embroider the facial features Ⓐ. Use a damp cloth to remove the marks.

2 Use spray fabric adhesive to adhere the fabric for the front hair to the doll. Use free-motion sewing to attach Ⓑ.

3 Pin the face/upper body template onto the stitched muslin piece, add a ¼-inch (6 mm) seam allowance, and cut around the shape. Adhere fabric for the back of the hair to the back of the doll's head, and stitch along the bottom edge of the hair to attach Ⓒ.

4 Embroider a scale motif on the front and back tail pieces using free-motion sewing with your machine Ⓓ. Stitch the star appliqués to the upper torso.

5 Align the bottom edge of the front muslin piece with the top edge of the front tail piece, right sides together, and stitch **(E)**. Repeat this step with the back muslin piece and back tail piece.

6 Lay the front and back with right sides together and stitch, leaving an opening for turning **(F)**. Clip and notch the curves and turn the doll right side out. Stuff the doll with polyester fiberfill, and use the ladder stitch to close the opening.

7 Stitch both arm pairs together, right sides facing, leaving the short ends open **(G)**. Notch the curves. Carefully turn the arms right side out and stuff with polyester fiberfill. Turn the raw edges of the arms under ¼ (6 mm). Attach the arms to the body with two buttons and strong thread or embroidery floss (see Rotating Joints, page 9) **(H)**. Finish the doll by using the cotton swab to apply the chalk to each cheek, and then tie the ribbon around her neck **(I)**.

EYES AND BROWS
Constructing faces is Danita's favorite part of doll making. "I usually make the faces to replicate the girls in my paintings, and since my style is not realistic, I think it's easier to do so." She advises others to not worry about making the face perfectly symmetrical, and to focus instead on the eyes and brows since these features give expression to the whole face.

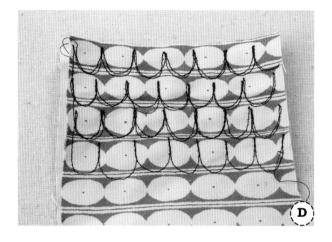

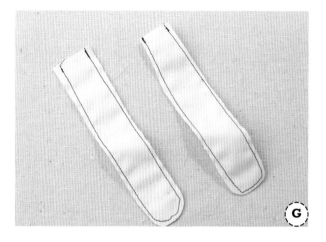

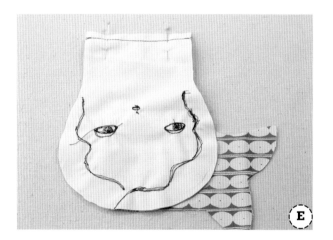

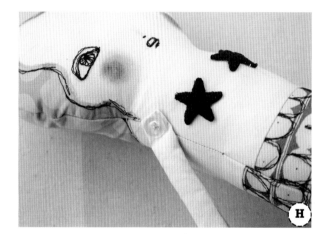

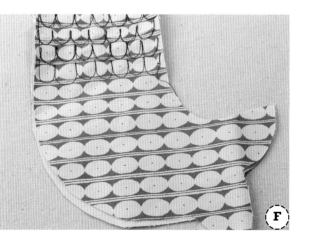

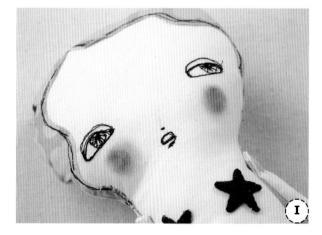

FRIDA

Her aim is to live a life filled with passion.

Before You Begin

Cut out the templates along the solid lines. Lay the face template on the muslin, trace around it, and set aside. Cut all other pieces of fabric by adding a ¼-inch (6 mm) seam allowance around each shape. Transfer all markings to the wrong side of the fabric.

What You Do

1 Mark the facial and hairline features on the traced muslin face using a water-soluble fabric marker. Thread your sewing machine with black thread, attach the darning foot, and lower the feed dogs. Use free-motion sewing to embroider all of the facial features. Remove the marks with a damp cloth.

2 Use spray fabric adhesive to adhere the felt for the hair around the face. Stitch along the edges to attach Ⓐ. Pin the face template on the stitched muslin piece, add a ¼-inch (6 mm) seam allowance, and cut around the shape.

RUN FORREST, RUN

Danita likes to shake things up when it comes to technique. What she does today will probably be different from what she'll be doing in two or three years. She describes herself as "kind of a Forrest Gump," the fictional character who ran and ran and ran until one day he just stopped. "It's the same for me. I'll try something new and do it and do it and do it until one day I just stop and move on to something else."

3 Use spray fabric adhesive to adhere the collar to the front of the body, then use free-motion sewing to stitch in place. Do the same for the rickrack trim at the waistline. Use free-motion sewing to embroider the row of buttons (B).

4 Align the bottom edge of the face with the top edge of the front of the body, right sides together, and stitch (C).

5 Stitch the legs with right sides together, clip the curves, turn, and stuff with polyester fiberfill. Make the arms in the same way (D). Align the raw edges of the legs with the bottom edge of the front body piece, right sides together, with the toes pointing toward the head (E). Pin and baste. Pin the back of the doll to the front with right sides together and sew, leaving an opening at the top of the head for turning. Clip the curves and turn. Stuff the doll with polyester fiberfill, then hand sew the opening with the ladder stitch to close.

6 Attach the arms to the body with two buttons and strong thread or embroidery floss (see Rotating Joints, page 9) (F). Use the cotton swab to apply the chalk to each cheek.

7 Wrap the chunky black yarn around two fingers to create three to four loops. Use black thread to hand stitch the loops to the top of the head. Continue making loops and stitching until the entire top portion of the head is filled with hair (G). Attach a crocheted flower or other embellishment to the head area. Make two small bows with black embroidery floss and hand stitch them to the ankles.

(A)

(B)

(C)

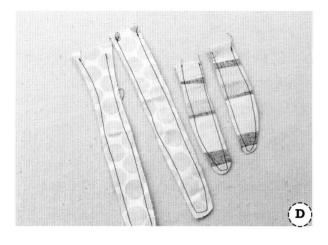

WOODLAND NYMPH

The grass is always greener for this adventure-loving woodland doll.

WHAT YOU'LL NEED

- Templates (pages 135–136)
- Doll Making Tool Kit (page 7)
- Red ticking, ¼ yard (.23 m)
- Muslin, 5 x 7 inches (12.7 x 17.8 cm)
- Print fabric, 8 x 5 inches (20.3 x 12.7 cm)
- Contrasting print or striped fabric, 8 x 13 inches (20.3 x 33 cm)
- Darning foot
- Black felt, 6 x 3 inches (15.2 x 7.6 cm)
- Lace ribbon, ¾ inch wide (1.9 cm), 6 inches (15.2 cm) long
- Pink velvet ribbon, ¼ inch wide (6 mm), 3½ inches (8.9 cm) long
- Green velvet ribbon, ¼ inch wide (6 mm), 6 inches (15.2 cm) long
- Rickrack, 6 inches (15.2 cm)
- Fabric for legs, 5 x 7 inches (12.7 x 17.8 cm)
- Fabric for arms, 6 x 6 inches (15.2 x 15.2 cm)
- Embroidery floss
- 2 buttons
- Strong thread
- Pink chalk
- Cotton swab
- Chunky black yarn, 1 skein
- Crocheted flower or other embellishment (optional)

FINISHED SIZE

- 15 inches (38.1 cm) tall

Before You Begin

Cut out the templates along the solid lines. Lay the face template on the muslin, trace around it, and set aside. Cut all other pieces of fabric by adding a ¼-inch (6 mm) seam allowance around each shape. Transfer all markings to the wrong side of the fabric.

What You Do

1 With the hairline and facial features provided on the template as a guide, mark these features on the muslin using a water-soluble fabric marker. Thread your sewing machine with black thread, attach the darning foot, and lower the feed dogs. Employ free-motion sewing to embroider the facial features then remove all marks with a damp cloth.

2 Using the template as a guide, cut six scallops from the black felt. Apply spray fabric adhesive to adhere them around the face, and then stitch in place (A). Pin the face template on the stitched muslin piece, add a ¼-inch (6 mm) seam allowance, and cut around the shape.

3 Adhere the pink velvet ribbon and lace to the shirt with spray fabric adhesive. Use free motion sewing to embroider scallops on the lace and the row of stitched "buttons" on the lace and velvet (B).

4 Align the lower edge of the face to the top edge of the shirt with right sides together and stitch (C). Line up the lower edge of the shirt and the top edge of the skirt with right sides together and stitch (D). Use spray fabric adhesive to adhere the green velvet ribbon on top of the shirt and skirt seam, and rickrack to the hem of the skirt. Stitch in place (E). Cut a motif from the shirt fabric and use free-motion sewing to stitch it to the skirt (F).

5 Sew the legs, notch the curves, turn, and stuff with polyester fiberfill. Make the arms in the same way (G). Align the raw edges of the legs with the bottom edge of the front body piece, right sides together, and toes pointing toward the head. Pin and baste (H). Pin the back of the doll to the front with right sides together and stitch, leaving an opening at the top of the head for turning. Clip the curves and turn. Stuff the doll with polyester fiberfill, then hand sew the opening with the ladder stitch to close.

6 Attach the arms to the body with two buttons and strong thread or embroidery floss (see Rotating Joints, page 9) (I). Use the cotton swab to apply the chalk to each cheek.

7 Wrap the chunky black yarn around three fingers multiple times and then tie securely in the middle. Cut the loops at either ends to make a pompom. Repeat to make two pompoms. Sew them to the doll's head. Attach a crocheted flower or other embellishment to the hair. Make two bows with embroidery floss. Stitch one to the bottom of each leg.

IN GOOD COMPANY

One of the dolls Danita still has from her childhood is a rag doll named Little Orphan Annie. She's been repaired countless times, and Danita even cut her hair short, hoping it would grow back. She believes childhood can be very lonely at times, but having dolls makes it easier. "They keep us company without rejection, without resentment. I think toys make us feel loved and accepted. Toys never say no to us."

(A)

(B)

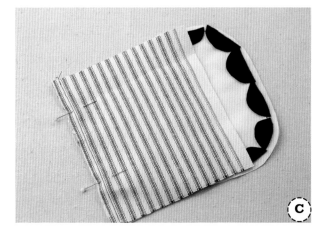

(C)

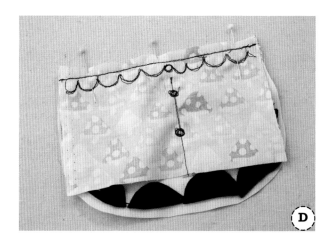

D

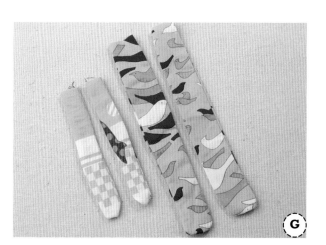

G

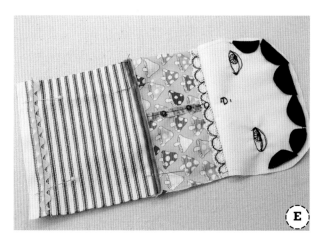

E

H

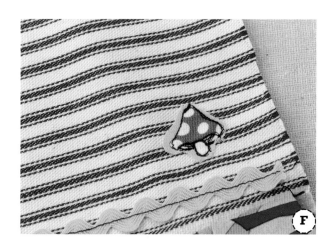

F

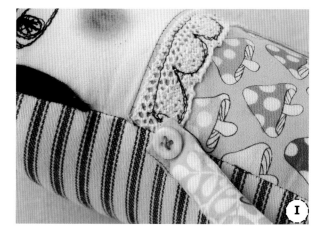

I

well. If Sasha isn't satisfied with the results, she will remake a doll—sometimes several times. And there isn't a technique or a color palette she's afraid to try, whether it's a red elephant, green rabbit, or pink frog.

Sasha's creative wish prompts her to make toys in even unfamiliar mediums. Her next big project involves working with papier-mâché, a technique Sasha wanted to learn. "I'm making a human-size doll for a movie. It's a huge crocodile that happens to be the best friend of the main character. I'm very thrilled, and I feel like I did when I made my first toy."

"I never say no to people. I know that I can do anything if I try. If I can't, I know I can learn." While Sasha is confident about her ability to hone new skills, she admits that sometimes mistakes do happen. Yet, she claims some of her best toys were created by accident. By combining unexpected materials, the end result can be gorgeous, and these otherwise "creative tragedies" always bring new ideas to her mind.

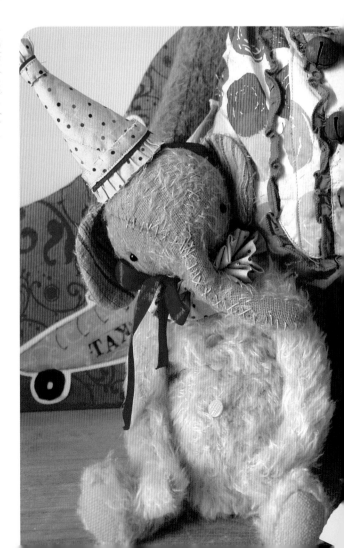

Sasha POKRASS

www.sashapokrass.etsy.com

Sasha Pokrass can't imagine her life without dolls—from first stitch to first hug, her toys are her life. "I love the idea that my toys will still be around 100 years from now when I'm not here." Sasha believes her toys create their own stories. One example comes from a man who bought a bear for his girlfriend. The bear went with the couple whenever they traveled, and they took pictures of it at every famous place. After two years, they lost the bear in the Crimea Mountains. The artist says of that bear, "He decided to end his travels and settle in one place. What better place for a bear than the mountains?"

A Piece of Energy

Sasha claims that you can see how an artist develops from toy to toy. "Like everything handmade, it's the charisma of the creator that makes a toy special. It's a piece of energy that people want to feel and have around, because every doll tells the story of its creator."

She enjoys taking a piece of fabric and seeing what it will become, and learning about where it will go. She particularly loves soft dolls because you not only look at them, but touch them and hold them as

Work and Play

A sudden impulse to try something new led eight-year-old Sasha to enroll in a doll-making workshop with a friend. She seemingly predicted her own future on that first day of class when she walked up to the instructor and declared she wanted to make dolls. She started making clowns, gnomes, African-style dolls, raindrops, parrots, and chickens. Eventually, she earned her own money by selling her toys to a toy store. Sasha was even able to pay for several trips to Moscow, where she appeared on TV shows, was featured in newspapers, and taught master classes.

Sasha stopped making dolls during her teenage years, but several years later she felt the urge to create a toy for a birthday present. After searching the Internet for a good bunny pattern, Sasha took a teddy bear course. Pretty soon, bear making became an expensive and addictive hobby. Half of her monthly salary went to mohair, eyes, joint discs, fabric, and books.

Because she travels frequently, Sasha's workspace moves from place to place. When she's at home, however, every corner of her house is put to good use. With two small kids around, Sasha carefully organizes her work area, and only works when she's not playing with her children. For Sasha, life really is all about combining work and play. She enjoys it all—the process, the results, the mistakes, and, of course, the dolls.

EXPERT TIP

Different textures found in different fabrics help add distinction to dolls. So even if you have your go-to fabrics that you love to use, I encourage you to always be on the lookout for different fabrics and to try them out. From suede to mohair to corduroy and more, there are lots of fabrics out there just waiting to be discovered!

MAGICIAN BEAR

This fuzzy bear is full of magic and charm. Joint discs attached with T-cotter pins (found in craft stores or online) allow you to move the bear's arms, legs, and head.

WHAT YOU'LL NEED

* Templates (pages 137–138)
* Doll Making Tool Kit (page 7)
* Cardboard or cardstock, 20 x 22 inches (50.8 x 55.9 cm)
* Faux fur or viscose fabric in a light color, ¼ yard (22.9 cm)
* Fuzzy or furry fabric for the vest, 10 x 5 (25.4 x 12.7 cm)
* Single-edge razor blade
* Awl
* Polyester fiberfill or wood wool (excelsior)
* 6 joint discs, 3 cm
* 4 joint discs, 2.5 cm
* 5 T-cotter pins, 28 mm
* Artificial sinew or waxed thread
* 2 light brown 2 mm glass eyes on wire loops
* Needle-nose pliers
* Glass beads or mineral granules
* Curved needle
* Black embroidery floss
* Beads and assorted embellishments

FINISHED SIZE

* 11 inches (27.9 cm) tall

Before You Begin

Trace the templates on the cardboard or cardstock and cut them out. A ¼-inch (6 mm) seam allowance is built into the templates. Trace the templates onto the wrong side of the fabrics, transferring all markings and notches. Trace the correct number, reversing the pieces as needed. Use a single-edge razor blade to cut the pattern pieces from the wrong side of the faux fur. Cut on traced pattern lines, through the backing only, then gently pull faux fur apart.

What You Do

1 Pin and stitch the two head pieces with right sides together, from the tip of the nose (a) to the edge of the neck (b). Pin the center of the muzzle (a) on the head gusset to the tip of the nose seam (a) on the head piece. Pin the back of the gusset (b) to the back edge of the neck (b) on each side. Stitch both sides of the gusset.

2 Pin the ear pieces with right sides together, and stitch. Clip the curves, turn, and whipstitch the openings closed.

3 Stitch the darts at the bottom of the body pieces. Pin and stitch the two body pieces with right sides together, aligning (d) and (e) points, leaving an opening for turning and stuffing (Ⓐ).

4 Pin the neck circle to the main body and stitch. Use the awl to make small holes at the joint points (indicated by the X marks on the pattern) for arms, legs, and center of the neck. Turn the body right side out (Ⓑ).

5 Pin the leg pieces with right sides together and stitch. Clip the curves and turn right side out. Make the arms in the same way.

6 Stuff the head firmly with polyester fiberfill or wood wool. Hand sew a gathering stitch along the neck edge of the head. Place a 3 cm joint disc on one of the cotter pins. Insert the disc into the neck opening (Ⓒ). Tightly pull the gathering stitches around the disc and tie off securely, taking extra stitches if necessary. Bury the knot. Whipstich the ears to the head.

7 Thread a glass eye onto a length of the artificial sinew or waxed thread (Ⓓ). Thread both ends through the eye of a doll needle. With the wire loop centered and standing straight up from the back of the glass eye, pinch the loop closed with needle-nose pliers. Insert the needle into the head at one of the eye points. Bring the needle out under the base of the neck (Ⓔ). Repeat for the second eye. Tightly pull the threads to sink the eyes, tie the threads together and bury the knots.

8 Attach the head by pushing the end of the cotter pin, extending from the head into the hole in the center of the neck circle (Ⓕ). Working from the inside of the body, place a 3 cm joint disc onto the cotter pin that is extending from the neck. Use the needle-nose pliers to bend and curl the ends of the cotter pin to secure the joint (Ⓖ).

9 Firmly stuff the bottom half of each arm. NOTE: I always stuff the body with polyester fiberfill or wood wool and glass beads or mineral granules to add weight and flexibility. If desired, you can do the same for the arms and legs. Use the awl to make a small hole at the joint marks.

10 Place a 2.5 cm joint disc onto a cotter pin and insert it into the arm, allowing the pin to go through the joint hole (**H**). Finish stuffing the arm, using a blanket stitch to close the opening. Repeat for the other arm. Repeat the same process for both legs, using 3 cm joint discs.

11 To join the limbs to the body, push the ends of the cotter pin extending from the limb into the corresponding joint hole on the body. From the inside of the body, place another joint disc onto the end of the pin. Use the needle-nose pliers to bend and curl the ends of the pin to secure the joint. Use 3 cm joint discs for the legs and 2.5 cm discs for the arms (**I**).

12 Stuff the body with polyester fiberfill or wood wool. If desired, stuff the lower part of the body with glass beads or mineral granules to add weight. Stitch the opening closed using the ladder stitch.

13 Use the curved needle with black embroidery floss to embroider the nose, mouth, and claws. Bury all knots to finish (**J**).

14 Make the vest by stitching the two front pieces of the vest to the back piece from (f) to (g), and then from (h) to (i). Attach beads or other embellishments on the front.

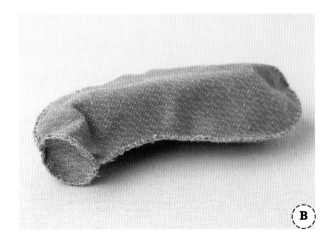

(**B**)

(**C**)

(**A**)

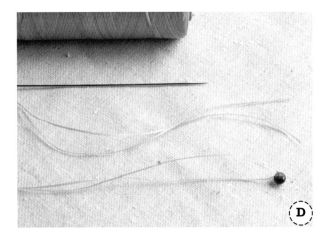

(**D**)

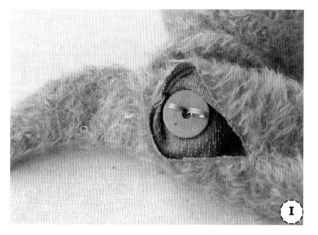

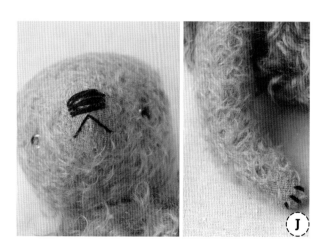

ELLY THE MAGIC ELEPHANT

This loveable, ambling pachyderm is ready to do the elephant walk.

WHAT YOU'LL NEED

* Templates (pages 139–140)
* Doll Making Tool Kit (page 7)
* Cardboard or cardstock, 20 x 22 inches (50.8 x 55.9 cm)
* Suede or viscose fabric, ¼ yard (.3 m)
* Awl
* Polyester fiberfill or wood wool (excelsior)
* 10 joint discs, 3 cm
* 5 T-cotter pins, 28 mm
* 2 light brown 6 mm glass eyes on wire loops
* Artificial sinew or waxed thread
* Needle-nose pliers
* Glass beads or mineral granules
* Curved needle
* 3 beads
* Thin ribbon, 2 pieces, each 6 inches (15.2 cm)
* Lace ribbon, 28 inches (71.1 cm)

FINISHED SIZE

* 12 inches (30.5 cm) tall

Before You Begin

Trace the templates on the cardboard or cardstock and cut them out. A ¼-inch (6 mm) seam allowance is built into the templates. Trace the templates on the wrong side of the fabric, transferring all markings and notches. Trace the correct number, reversing the pieces as needed.

What You Do

1 Pin and sew the two head pieces with right sides together, from the top front of the nose (a) to the front edge of the neck (c).

2 Pin the nose of the gusset (a) to the top front of the nose (a) on the head gusset. Pin the back of the gusset (b) to the back edge of the neck on each side of the head. Stitch from (a) to (b) on both sides of the gusset.

3 Pin the ear pieces with right sides together and stitch. Clip the curves, turn right side out, and whipstitch the openings closed.

4 Stitch the darts at the bottom of the body pieces. Pin and stitch the two body pieces with right sides together, leaving an opening for turning and stuffing Ⓐ. Pin the neck circle to the main body lining up (d) and (e) and stitch.

5 Use the awl to make a small hole at the joint points for the arms and the legs, and in the center of the neck circle. Turn the body right side out.

6 Pin the arm pieces with right sides together, and stitch. Clip the curves, turn right side out, and set aside.

7 Pin the pieces for one leg with right sides together. Stitch the leg together, leaving the end of the leg open. Pin the footpad at the front toe and back heel points (f) and (g) to secure. Whipstitch around the entire foot, easing the footpad to fit. Repeat for the second leg (B). Clip the curves, and turn right side out.

8 Stuff the head firmly with small wads of polyester fiberfill or wood wool. Add glass beads or mineral granules when stuffing the trunk to give more weight and flexibility. Sew a gathering stitch by hand along the neck edge of the head. Place a joint disc on a T-cotter pin. Insert the disc into the neck opening. Tightly pull the gathering stitches around the disc and tie off securely, taking extra stitches if necessary (C). Bury the knot. Whipstitch the ears to the head.

9 Thread a glass eye onto a length of sinew or waxed thread, then thread both ends of the thread through the eye of a doll needle. With the wire loop centered and standing straight up from the back of the glass eye, pinch the loop closed using the needle-nose pliers. Insert the needle into the head at one of the eye points, bring it out under the base of the neck. Repeat for the second eye. Tightly pull the threads to sink the eyes. Tie the threads for each of the eyes together and bury the knots.

10 Attach the head. Push the end of the cotter pin extending from the head into the hole in the center of the neck circle. Working from the inside of the body, insert a joint disc on the cotter pin coming through the neck. Use the needle-nose pliers to bend and curl the ends of the cotter pin to secure the joint (D).

11 Firmly stuff an arm below the opening with polyester fiberfill. NOTE: I always stuff the body with filling and glass beads or mineral granules to add weight and flexibility. If desired, you can do the same for the arms and legs. Use the awl to make a small hole at the joint mark.

12 Place a joint disc onto a cotter pin and insert it into the arm, allowing the pin to go through the joint hole. Finish stuffing the arm, using a blanket stitch to close the opening, and then repeat for the other arm (E). Repeat the same process for both legs.

13 To join the limbs to the body, push the ends of the cotter pin extending from the limb into the corresponding joint hole on the body (F). From the inside of the body, place another joint disc onto the end of the pin. Use the needle-nose pliers to bend and curl the ends of the pin to secure the joint.

14 Stuff the lower part of the body with glass beads or mineral granules to add weight to the doll. Stuff the remainder of the body with polyester fiberfill or wood wool.

15 Stitch three beads to the center front of the elephant using a curved needle and thread. Bury the knots.

16 Hand sew one piece of thin ribbon to one end of the lace ribbon. Run a gathering stitch through the center of the lace ribbon. Pull the thread to gather the lace to approximately 6 inches (15.2 cm). Hand sew the remaining piece of thin ribbon to the other end of the gathered lace ribbon. Tie this collar around the elephant's neck (G).

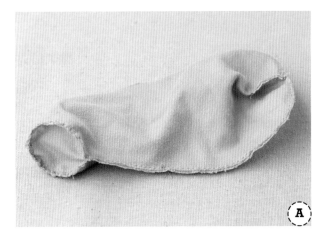

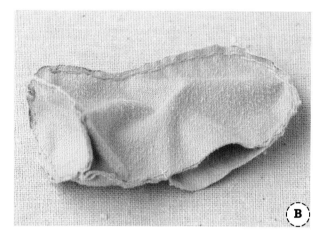

B

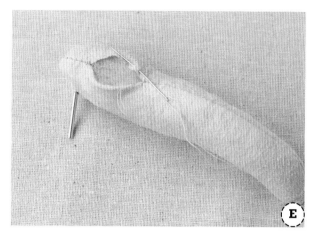

E

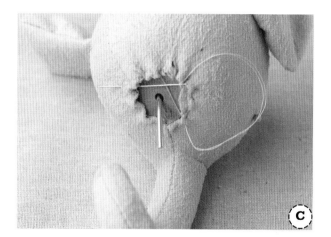

C

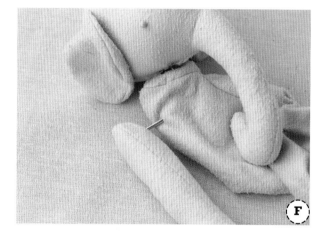

F

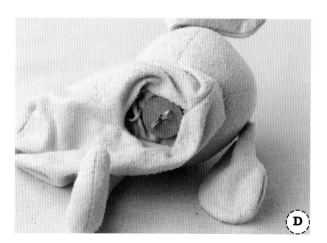

D

G

LITTLE MISS MINI

Take this diminutive doll wherever you go. Because she's all ears, she's one friend who'll listen to your every word.

WHAT YOU'LL NEED

* Template (page 138)
* Doll Making Tool Kit (page 7)
* Cardboard or cardstock, 20 x 22 inches (50.8 x 55.9 cm)
* Scraps of orange and white fabric
* Curved needle
* Black embroidery floss
* 2 black seed beads
* 2 white sequins
* 3 amber seed beads
* 3 gold sequins
* Lace ribbon, 10 inches (25.4 cm)
* Thin ribbon, 6 inches (15.2 cm)
* Pin back (optional)

FINISHED SIZE

* 5 inches (12.7 cm) tall

Before You Begin

Trace the templates on the cardboard or cardstock and cut them out. Transfer all markings on pattern for openings. In the following steps, use the templates as follows: Fold fabric in half, right sides together. Place templates on the wrong side of the fabric and trace around. Stitch on the drawn lines, leaving openings for turning. Cut out *after* sewing, leaving a ¼-inch (6 mm) seam allowance. Clip the curves, turn right side out.

What You Do

1 Stitch the head as described above (A). Clip the curves, turn right side out. Firmly stuff with small wads of polyester fiberfill and hand stitch the opening closed (B).

2 Run a gathering stitch by hand around the edge of the muzzle. Place a very small piece of polyester fiberfill in the center. Gently pull the threads to gather, and then secure by tying off the threads.

3 Determine the desired position for the muzzle on the face, and then use the curved needle to sew it in place. Embroider the nose with the curved needle, black embroidery floss, and simple stitches.

4 Make the eyes by stitching the black seed beads on top of the white sequins with the black floss (C). Bury all knots.

THE RIGHT LOOK

Even though it takes Sasha many tries before finding the right look for her dolls, she admits they usually end up looking like her or her kids!

5 Stitch the ears, clip the curves, and turn right side out. Lightly stuff the ears with polyester fiberfill and sew them to the back of the head near the top seam **(D)**.

6 Stitch the body, clip the curves, and turn right side out. Firmly stuff with polyester fiberfill. Whipstitch the opening closed and hand sew the body to the head **(E)**.

7 Stitch the arms and legs, clip the curves, and turn right side out. Firmly stuff with polyester fiberfill, whipstitch the openings closed.

8 Sew the arms and legs on the body, running the needle all the way through a joint on one side of the body, and then through the joint on the other side **(F)**. Bury all knots. On the front of the body, stitch the amber seed beads on top of the gold sequins.

9 Run a gathering stitch through the center of the lace ribbon from end to end. Pull the thread to gather the lace, and then sew it to the neck area. Add the thinner ribbon to the center of the neck, and tie it into a bow. NOTE: If you would like to wear the bunny as a brooch, stitch a small pin to its back.

THE HIGH PRICE OF MAKING DOLLS

Sasha's number one critic is her husband. "He has an innate sense of taste and always tells me his opinion once the toy is ready." Sasha completely trusts him because he's always been right over the years. Her son loves everything she does. "He gives hugs to the toys and likes to dance with them. He especially likes toys that are bigger than him."

A

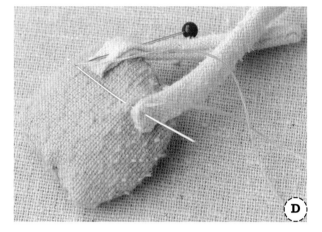

D

B

E

C

F

Mimi KIRCHNER
www.mimikirchner.com

Mimi Kirchner's creations are one part self-portrait (yes, all of them), and one part the friends she wishes she had. "And every once in a while I make a doll that I fall in love with—there's something just right about it. And then, I want to capture that feeling again," says Mimi.

Down the Rabbit Hole

The concept of falling describes all of Mimi's experiences with art. "When I get interested in something, I don't do it halfway. I think in terms of falling into a well or down the rabbit hole." Mimi first fell for pottery, and figurative art always attracted her. She found the challenge of fitting an illustrated figure onto a piece of functional tableware appealing.

Then in 2000, Mimi was swept off her feet when she was helping her mother-in-law dress some antique dolls. The experience opened her eyes to many different types of dolls. When she became the recipient of her mom's vast stash of fine fabrics and sewing supplies, she decided to take the plunge.

While Mimi had made dolls as gifts for her kids, she realized she needed to be at a place in life where she felt comfortable with herself as an artist in the medium, "Because, honestly, no one else is going to take you seriously when you tell them you're a doll artist!" Mimi, however, doesn't take herself completely seriously. When comparing her childhood creativity to now, she said she used to make doll clothes out of old and unmatched socks and hasn't "come too far from that!"

Catalyst for Imagination

In her childhood art collection, Mimi had a drawer full of paper dolls which represented the many hours she spent with scissors in hand. Though she's moved to soft dolls, Mimi still relies on her trusty scissors. Soft dolls "have an echo of childhood for many people," says Mimi. She describes these plush dolls as being warm, and when made with reclaimed materials, the fabrics have their own story.

But that doesn't mean Mimi's dolls alone don't have stories to tell. In fact, Mimi prefers that the people looking at her dolls create the stories for them. "The dolls will be a catalyst for the imagination. No static story lines. I absolutely love when people tell me who they think my dolls are. It always makes me feel successful when my work creates a spark."

Community

Mimi enjoys "solving all the little problems that come up with every doll," and it's this particular challenge of doll making that keeps Mimi hooked. "Once I have it all figured out, it's no longer interesting." Her work includes sharing via her blog and Flickr. Mimi thrives on the feedback because her fans can share with her as well. "I need to know that people are looking, and enjoying, and getting it."

Because Mimi cares so much about interaction, she considers herself not just a part of the doll community, but something bigger. "When I put my first pattern out into the world (Purl Soho Girl) I had no idea how emotional I would become when I saw the dolls people made. It's like sending a child out into the world and watching them flourish!"

TATTOOE' MAN

When ink looks this good, tattoos have no taboo. And there's no need to fear the needle—these tats are made of toile.

3 Pin and
togethe
cente
ed

WHAT YOU'LL NEED

* Templates (pages 141–143)
* Doll Making Tool Kit (page 7)
* White quilting-weight cotton, ¼ yard (.23 m)
* Black quilting-weight cotton, ⅛ yard (11.4 cm)
* 1 fat quarter of a small-scale cotton toile
* 1 fat quarter of striped quilting-weight cotton
* Dye bath (optional)
* Paper stencil (see Creating Facial Stencils on page 56)
* Black and red embroidery floss and needle
* Black ribbon, ⅜-inch (1 cm) wide, 10 inches (25.4 cm)
* 1 small decorative button

FINISHED SIZE

* 16 inches (40.6 cm) tall

Before You Begin

Cut out all templates along the solid lines, then cut the shapes from fabric. A ¼-inch (6 mm) seam allowance is built into all templates. When cutting the pants, lay the inner leg of the template along a stripe. Transfer all markings to the wrong side of the fabric. NOTE: You may want to dye the white cotton and the toile to give the fabric an antique look. Prepare a simple dye bath by steeping four black tea bags in 1 cup (250 ml) of hot water for approximately three minutes. Alternatively, you can mix ¼ tsp. (1 ml) of tan liquid dye in 1 quart (.9 l) of hot water with 1 tbsp. (14 g) of salt.

What You Do

1 If you're dyeing the fabric, dye before cutting pattern pieces. Soak the fabric in the prepared dye bath and dry flat. Iron the fabric before cutting into pattern pieces.

2 With right sides together, match, pin, and stitch the front of the head to the chest front at the neck, the waist of the chest to the waist of the pants, and the front of the boots to the bottom pants leg. Do the same for the back of the body back, leaving an opening for turning as marked on the template Ⓐ.

MIRROR IMAGE

Mimi spends time designing her faces, each of which is unique. She works to achieve the correct placement of the features that allows everything else to fall in the right place. If the sketch doesn't look right, Mimi holds it up to the mirror, which, she claims, quickly reveals the problem. Once Mimi creates a successful design for a face, she makes a simple template.

stitch the hands to the arms with right sides
[together], then press open. Fold the joined piece down the
[center], matching seams at the wrist (B). Stitch the outer
[edge], leaving an opening as marked on the template. Trim
the seam allowance ⅛ inch (3 mm), clip the curves, and turn
right side out (C).

4 Lay the body front on the body back with right sides
together. Align the edges, and pin carefully to match all
seams. Stitch the front to the back, and then clip the curves
before turning right side out. Make sure all the seams are
pushed out, and flatten the body.

5 Use the water-soluble fabric marker to mark the inside
leg line. Stitch the marked leg line up from the feet, and
then back down again (D).

6 Draw the facial features and back hairline, using the
prepared paper stencils (see Creating Facial Stencils), and
the water-soluble fabric marker (E).

7 Stuff the body and the arms firmly with polyester
fiberfill. Use a pointed utensil to make sure the ankles and
wrists are well stuffed. When finished, the doll should be
able to stand on its own. Fold in the seam allowances at the
openings, and hand sew closed. Set the arms aside.

8 Embroider the facial features with the embroidery floss
and needle. Use the stem stitch for the eyebrows and nose,
and to outline the hair and mustache, the satin stitch for the
lips and eyes, and the seed stitch or satin stitch to fill in the
hair and mustache as desired (F).

9 Attach the black ribbon around the waist seam with
spray fabric adhesive. Overlap at the center front, and hand
sew in place. Sew the button for the buckle at the center
front to cover the overlap.

10 Attach the arms. Using needle and thread, anchor
several strands of thread in the shoulder of the doll. Then
take the same thread through the shoulder point of the
body. Do not pull the thread to tighten the arm all the way
to the body, but pass through several times, making sure the
stitches are loose enough to allow movement. Finish with
several tiny anchor stitches under the arm. Repeat for the
other arm (G).

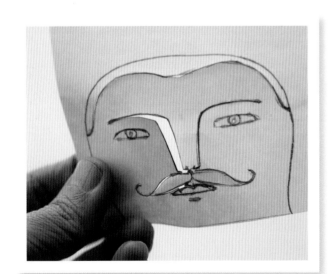

CREATING FACIAL STENCILS
You can purchase stencil paper to make the stencils,
but freezer paper that can be found in the grocery store
works as well. Once the features are drawn, use a sharp
craft knife to cut very narrow slits along the lines. Be
sure to leave just enough paper attached where needed to
keep your stencil together. To stencil the features on the
fabric, just slip the point of a water-soluble fabric marker
through the cut slits and trace.

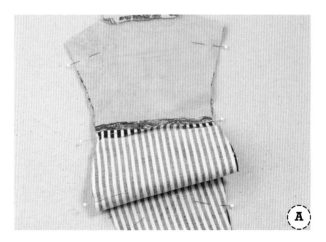

(A)

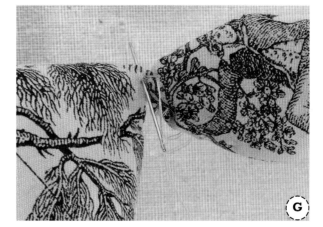

SWEATER BABY

From head to toe, this doll is cradled in the warmth of felt. The soft and squishy body and sweet little face make it a perfect gift for welcoming a new baby.

WHAT YOU'LL NEED

- Templates (pages 144–145)
- Doll Making Tool Kit (page 7)
- 2 pieces of felt from a felted sweater, each 10 x 12 inches (25.4 x 30.5 cm)
- Flesh-tone wool felt, 3 x 2½ inches (7.6 x 6.4 cm)
- Wool or felt for mittens, 8 x 2 inches (20.3 x 5.1 cm)
- Scraps of wool or felt
- Thread to match felt
- Paper stencil (see Creating Facial Stencils on page 56)
- Embroidery floss in assorted colors and needle

FINISHED SIZE

- 9 inches (22.9 cm) tall

Before You Begin

Cut out all templates along the solid lines then cut out the shapes from the fabrics. A ¼-inch (6 mm) seam allowance is built into the body and mitten templates and the top edge of the flower appliqué. Based on the bulkiness of the felt you use, you may need to cut a larger seam allowance. For the appliqués, pin the templates on the felt and cut along the solid lines.

What You Do

1 Stitch each of the mittens together, leaving the wrist edges open. Clip the curves and turn right side out. Stuff the mittens with a small amount of the polyester fiberfill. Do not overfill; you want them to be fairly flat (A).

2 Stitch the front and back body with right sides together. Leave openings at each wrist and at the crotch (B). Do not turn.

3 Insert the mittens into the doll arms, aligning the raw edges. Make sure the thumbs are aligned with the top edge of the arm. Stitch in place. Clip or notch the curves, and turn the body right side out.

4 Use a water-soluble fabric marker to mark the hip and shoulder stitch lines and the face placement on the front of the doll.

5 Stuff the doll lightly with polyester fiberfill. The doll should be soft and approximately 2 inches (5.1 cm) thick at the tummy area after stuffing. Hand sew the crotch opening closed (C).

6 Sew the hip and shoulder lines by hand. With a double strand of the sewing thread and using the running stitch, sew up and down through the doll, as if you were hand quilting (D). Make several stitches at the beginning and end of each section to anchor the stitches in place.

7 Make the facial stencils following the instructions in Creating Facial Stencils on page 56. Trace the facial features from the stencil onto the flesh-tone felt face.

8 Use the stem stitch to outline the nose with rust embroidery floss. Use the satin stitch with white floss to embroider across the eyes, and blue floss to embroider down the center of the eyes for the pupils. Embroider the mouth using the satin stitch and red floss (E).

9 Pin the appliqués, including the face, to the front of the doll. Use the overcast stitch to attach the flower and leaf appliqués to each other and to the doll (F).

10 Overcast stitch the face onto the doll. With a double strand of sewing thread and using the running stitch, sew between the marked dots around the top half of the head (G).

11 With either the stem stitch or chain stitch, embroider the stem and the details on the leaves (H). Use a damp cloth to remove any lines left by the marker.

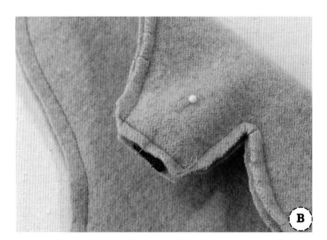

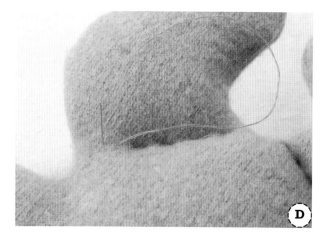

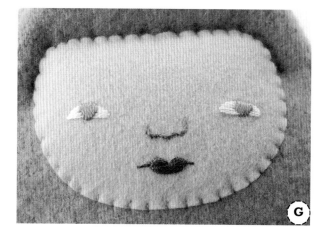

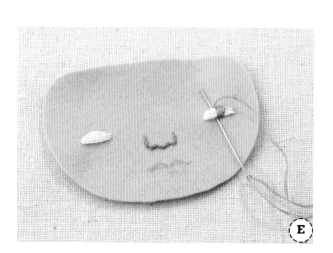

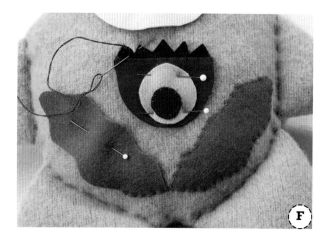

A DESK OF MY OWN

Years ago, Mimi took her son to a talk given by author and illustrator Philip Pullman. One of the things he talked about was that people often ask where he gets his ideas. As she recalls, he said something along the lines of, "the ideas come to my desk and if I'm there, I get them. If I'm not, I don't." Mimi loves this explanation and agrees that, "so much of art is just being at your desk."

Trial and error have since prevailed as Maria's creative philosophy. The artist points out that drawing, sewing, quilting, and embroidery all require periods of experimental work. "Many of the skills that I have were born from persistence; from giving myself completely to projects that might not turn out that well."

Currently, her workroom is the largest room in her house and contains three sewing machines. "I'm very methodical and organized. Everything is in the right place," says the artist, who doesn't believe in wasting precious creative time looking for supplies. The room is divided into three main areas where you'll find drawing boards, computers, a fabric and papers cabinet, and small white boxes clearly labelled for buttons and ribbons. There's even an area dedicated to recreation, complete with sofas and a television.

While she works, Maria listens to her favorite music, or sometimes just listens to the silence of the countryside. Music and the sounds of nature are Maria's only key ingredients for a productive day. "Working alone at home requires a big inner discipline. I usually work in the afternoon so I can enjoy the daylight."

Maria MADEIRA
www.kase-faz.bigcartel.com

For an artist who describes herself as restless by nature, Maria Madeira likes to constantly shake things up—a concept that excites her and her fans as well. In fact, the big idea behind her business, kase-faz, is that Maria can constantly change her product and means of expression. In doing so, Maria keeps her work contemoraneous and diverse.

Trial and Error

For Maria, making dolls is all about the magic of going back to childhood. "I remember drawing as a child and dressing the dolls that I made," she recalls. Even then she was attracted to the colors of fabric. Her memories include her fascination with the small textile factory she would pass on her way home from school.

Maria has experimented with many mediums in art and craft production. In 2005, when the art and crafts movement became big, she decided, with the support of her husband, to move forward with her business. She stitched her first doll completely by hand, and, soon after, bought a sewing machine without ever looking back.

A Blank Page

Regardless of when and where she creates, Maria believes that each doll is a blank page that comes to life as she makes them. Their story begins in the studio and ends elsewhere, hopefully within someone else's arms. Maria can never say for sure how a doll's story will end. But she says she'll count herself successful when mothers pass her dolls down to their daughters.

Getting her work out is important to Maria, and receiving feedback is vital to her growth as an artist. That's why she shares her work through her blog, Flickr, and Facebook. It's the bond between mothers and daughters, artist and buyer, creator and creation that drives her work—and generates the special magic you feel when you see one of her dolls.

EXPERT TIP

To become a better dollmaker: observe, learn, and practice techniques from other creative disciplines. Methods found in the world of quilting, for example, can open up new ideas on how to create a doll's body.

JOSEFINA

Don't feel sorry for little sleepy-eyed Josefina. She's the ideal companion for any sleepy head in your life.

WHAT YOU'LL NEED

- ✳ Templates (pages 146–147)
- ✳ Doll Making Tool Kit (page 7)
- ✳ White muslin for the face, 5 x 5 inches (12.7 x 12.7 cm)
- ✳ Batting, 12 x 14 inches (30.5 x 35.6 cm)
- ✳ White muslin for the body, 10 x 5 inches (25.4 x 12.7 cm)
- ✳ Blue felt, 5 x 8 inches (12.7 x 20.3 cm)
- ✳ Red and blue fabric scraps
- ✳ Black and red embroidery floss and needle
- ✳ 2 white buttons
- ✳ Upholstery thread
- ✳ Hook and eye
- ✳ Lace trim, 7½ inches (19 cm)

FINISHED SIZE

- ✳ 16 inches (40.6 cm) tall

Before You Begin

Cut out all templates along the solid lines, then trace them onto the wrong side of the fabrics. When you cut the fabric, add a ¼-inch (6 mm) seam allowance around each shape. Cut a front and back body from both the muslin and batting, then adhere each batting piece to a muslin piece using the spray adhesive.

What You Do

1 Cut two matching strips from each of the assorted red and blue fabrics. Pin them across the front and back body pieces in matching rows that overlap by ¼ inch (6 mm). Stitch the rows in place along the horizontal edges, and add quilting lines as you like. Trim the ends of the strips to the shape of the body, and baste around the perimeter (**A**).

2 Fold under the bottom edge of the muslin face and adhere the piece to the top of the front body with fabric spray adhesive. Stitch the bottom edge and edgestitch around the sides. Mark the facial features with a water-soluble fabric marker and embroider the features using the black and red embroidery floss. To create the nose, roll up a small piece of polyester fiberfill and stitch it onto the face using multiple up-and-down stitches.

3 Pin the ear pairs together with right sides together and stitch, leaving the straight end open. Clip the curves and turn them right side out. Edgestitch around the curved edge of each ear. Align the raw edges of the ears with the raw edges of the front of the head, per the template placement marks, with right sides together. Pin and baste (**B**).

4 Pin the leg pairs with right sides together and stitch, leaving the straight end open. Clip the curves, turn right side out, and stuff (**C**). NOTE: The leg template does not include the accent feet. If desired, make smaller feet templates by using the end of the leg template as a guide.

5 Align the raw edges of the legs with the bottom edge of the front body piece, right sides together, with toes pointing toward the head. Pin and baste. Pin the back of the doll to the front with right sides together and stitch, leaving the top portion of the head open for turning. Turn the doll right side out and stuff. Sew the opening closed.

6 Stitch the two hair bun pieces with right sides together, clip the curves, turn right side out, and stuff. Align the raw edge of the hair bun to the top edge of the front hair piece, right sides together. Pin and baste. Pin the back side of the hair piece to the front with right sides together and sew. Turn right side out. Using a needle and embroidery floss, attach the entire hair piece on the doll's head with an overcast stitch (D).

7 Pin the arm pairs with right sides together, and stitch. Clip the curves, turn, and stuff. Sew the openings closed and attach them to the body with two small buttons, using the doll needle and upholstery thread (E) (see Rotating Joints, page 9). Attach one arm, and then pass the needle and thread through the body to attach the other arm. Sew red felt patches to the doll's elbows.

8 Pin the two collar pieces with right sides together, and stitch. Clip the curves, and turn right side out. Do the same with the remaining cape pieces. Insert the raw edges of the collar in between the lining and front of the cape, turn the raw edges of the cape under, and topstitch in place. Sew a hook and eye in place (F).

9 Hand stitch a length of lace at the bottom of the doll for the skirt. Sew the boots, clip the curves, turn them right side out, and put them on the doll.

10 Create and attach additional embellishments for the collar area as desired (G).

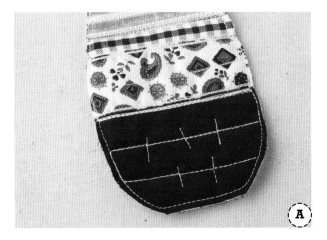

(A)

(B)

(C)

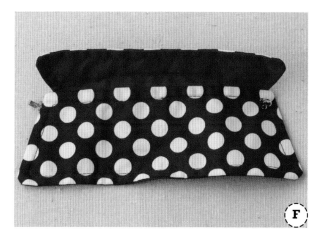

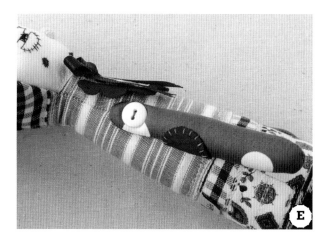

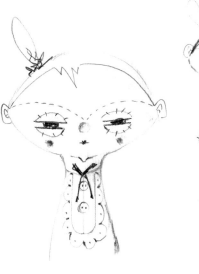

Character Dolls

Once you create Josefina using the templates provided, I encourage you to try your hand at developing your own character doll by first sketching the figure, and then creating corresponding templates. To develop Josefina, I used a pencil and paper to sketch concepts from my imagination of how I wanted the doll to look. Shown here are the preliminary sketches I made to create her. From there, I drafted templates. The easiest way to do this is to fold paper in half and draw half the figure on it. When you cut out the template and open the paper, both sides will be exactly the same. You can create your own animal dolls as well by observing and sketching different animal characteristics, as I did for Bobi Dog on page 68.

BOBI DOG

This playful pup is front and center for fun and action. His floppy ears and bright button eyes make it hard to avoid love at first sight.

WHAT YOU'LL NEED

* Templates (pages 148–149)
* Doll Making Tool Kit (page 7)
* Wool suiting, ¼ yard (22.9 cm)
* Fabric scraps for ears
* Fabric scraps for legs
* Brown felt scraps
* 2 white buttons
* Dark brown embroidery floss and needle
* Hemp thread
* 4 brown buttons
* 1 small felt ball
* Ribbon, 1-inch (2.5 cm) wide, 27 inches (68.6 cm)

FINISHED SIZE

* 11 inches (27.9 cm) long

Before You Begin

Cut out all templates along the solid lines. When you cut the fabric, add a ¼-inch (6 mm) seam allowance around each shape.

What You Do

1 Sew the brown felt eye patches onto both sides of the head and the spots onto both sides of the body. Attach white buttons for the eyes, and then embroider accents around the eye patches and spots using dark brown embroidery floss **(A)**.

2 Pin the ear pieces with right sides together and stitch. Clip or notch the curves, and turn right side out. Add ¼ inch (6 mm) around the ear. On narrow end of the ear, fold side seams toward the center and baste.

3 Stack the ears with right sides together. Pin them in position to the right side of one of the body pieces. Align the raw edges, pointing the lobes toward the belly of the dog. Baste in place through all layers.

4 Pin the tail pieces with right sides together, and stitch. Clip or notch the curves, turn right side out, and stuff with polyester fiberfill. Pin the tail in position to the right side of one of the body pieces. Align the raw edges, pointing the tip of the tail up toward the center of the dog.

ORGANIZATION PLUS

True to Maria's meticulous storage methods, her large stash of fabrics is organized and cross-organized. She starts with source first: American, Japanese, Portuguese, etc. She then cross references by type: cotton, wool, and mixed fabrics. Lastly, she divides by patterns, such as floral, stripes, and dots. No scrap of fabric, no matter how small, is thrown away; she even has a special stash for the tiniest of textiles.

5 Pin the two sides of the dog with right sides together and stitch, leaving an opening at the bottom for turning **(B)**. Clip the curves, turn the dog right side out, and stuff. Hand sew the opening closed **(C)**.

6 Pin the legs with right sides together and stitch, leaving an opening for turning. Clip the curves and turn right side out. Stuff, and then sew the openings closed **(D)**.

7 Double a strand of hemp thread. Thread both ends into the hole of a brown button, leave a ½-inch (1.3 cm) tail, and knot. Thread the loop of the doubled strand through the eye of the doll needle. Attach one leg, then pass the needle through the body to attach the other leg. Remove the needle, cut the loop, and then thread the two loose ends into the holes of another brown button. Pull the threads to tighten and knot; then cut, leaving a ½-inch (1.27 cm) tail. Repeat for the remaining set of legs **(E)** (see Rotating Joints, page 9).

8 Sew the small felt ball for the nose to the tip of the face **(F)**. Tie the length of ribbon around the dog's neck.

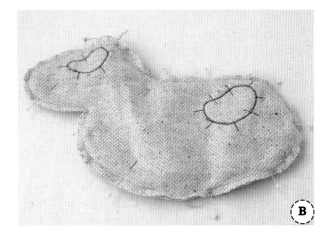

Character Dolls

Once you create Bobi Dog using the templates provided, I encourage you to try your hand at developing your own animal doll. Sketch the animal first, and then create corresponding templates. This is the preliminary sketch that I made for Bobi Dog, which consists of a one large part for the body and head, and then smaller parts for the ears and limbs. The key to designing animal dolls is to keep it simple.

BREAK TIME

Fabrics, with their potential for unlimited combinations, are the starting point for any work Maria does. When a new fabric order arrives, she immediately begins outlining how to transform it into works of art. She also finds the unique qualities of recycled textiles help her create visual stories when making character dolls. When inspiration lags, Maria usually takes a break. "Stopping for a while is very important for clearing your ideas and regaining energy. Inspiration can show up anytime."

Ana
FERNANDES
www.pinknounou.com

When you pick up an Ana Fernandes' creation, the feeling's almost as joyous as the one Ana has when she completes a doll. The meaning she finds in making her "softies" drives her creative process. Her love of warm, strong colors, textures, and shapes goes into each and every one of her signature dolls.

Trying, Trying, Trying

Ana's handprint is literally on every stitch of every piece she produces. She not only completes her dolls with hand embroidery and stitching, but also sometimes hand-printed fabrics. If possible, Ana would like to get even more hands-on by incorporating screen printing and traditional Portuguese embroidery in her work—and pretty much anything else that's arts and crafts related. "Once you learn a technique, you can always apply it from one area to another."

Learning is especially enjoyable for this fearless experimenter. "Trying, trying, trying" is Ana's mantra, and reading books is a favorite method of study. Her learning comes through technique-based books, but also through her passion for children's books. She considers her collection, *Softies and Tales*, which features fabric characters from classic children's stories, one of her greatest achievements.

While Ana's mother taught her some of the crafts she now embraces, she admits that she hasn't always had a love affair with needle and thread. "Very few people know that I didn't like sewing when I was young." But that doesn't mean she wasn't busy creating, even then. Ana was drawing at a young age, as well as cutting up pieces of fabric, playing with dolls, and piling up little pieces of wood that her father gave her from his furniture projects. Today, Ana continues to dabble in many mediums, creating baby accessories, bags, home décor, and fabric jewelry.

Everything in Its Place

Ana first makes a mental sketch before transforming it into something others can grab and feel. "I have a story in my head and on paper for each doll." With so many ideas and visions happening at once, it's important for Ana to stay organized. Her creative space is all about keeping fabrics, ribbons, felts, and other supplies in their proper location. Finished dolls and fabrics reside in a closet.

Everything is cut at the computer table. Above the computer area is a shelf with mementos and small materials. In another room with more light, Ana's sewing machine waits eagerly for its next project. On rainy days you'll find Ana's space soaked in candlelight. But rain or shine, you'll find this dollmaker steeped in silence (save for calming music) hard at work—most likely drawing up a mental storm.

ESTEFANIA

Which came first? Purple hair or purple boots?
Only Estefania knows!

WHAT YOU'LL NEED

* Templates (pages 150–151)

* Doll Making Tool Kit (page 7)

* White linen, ¼ yard (22.9 cm)

* Large polka-dotted fabric for body,
  6 x 8 inches (15.2 x 20.3 cm)

* Dark purple felt for hair, 9 x 12 inches
  (22.9 x 30.5 cm)

* Small polka-dotted fabric for arms,
  8 x 5 inches (20.3 x 12.7 cm)

* Light purple felt for legs,
  one 8-inch (20.3 cm) square

* Pink ribbon, ¾-inch (1.9 cm) wide,
  5 inches (12.7 cm) long

* Trim scraps (optional)

* Pink patterned fabric,
  16 x 4½ inches (40.6 x 11.4 cm)

* Striped elastic, ½-inch (1.3 cm) wide,
  7 inches (17.8 cm) long

* Embroidery floss in pink and gray

* Small pompom

FINISHED SIZE

* 14 inches (35.6 cm) tall

Before You Begin

Cut out the templates along the solid lines. When you cut the fabric, add a ¼ inch (6 mm) seam allowance around each shape. Transfer all markings to the wrong side of the fabric.

The arms and legs are designed to be cut from a single fabric; there are no separate templates for hands or boots. However, as shown on the doll, you can create hands and boots by stitching two fabrics together before cutting the template shapes.

What You Do

1 Embroider the facial features on the white linen face with pink and gray embroidery floss. Use a short running stitch for the mouth and to outline the cheeks and use a satin stitch to fill in the eyes (A).

2 Pin and stitch the pink ribbon and a scrap of the white linen fabric to the front body to create the neckline (B). Then, with right sides together and edges aligned, pin the top of the front body to the bottom of the face and stitch (C).

3 Pin the two back body pieces along one of their long edges with right sides together. Leave the opening for stuffing as indicated on the template. With right sides together and edges aligned, pin the top edge of the back body piece to the bottom edge of the back of the head and sew.

4 With right sides together, pin and stitch the arms, making sure to leave small openings for turning. Fold the leg pieces lengthwise, right sides together, pin, and sew, leaving small openings for stuffing. Clip the curves and turn.

5 With the front of the doll right side up, position the legs with toes pointing toward the head, raw edges aligned at the body bottom. Position the arms with raw edges aligned at the sides and hands pointing down. Pin and baste (D).

6 Place the back of the doll on the front with right sides together. Stitch the front to the back, trim the seam allowances, clip at the curves, and turn right side out through the back opening. Stuff the arms and legs through their small openings, and then whipstitch them closed. Stuff the rest of the doll and stitch the opening closed.

7 Embellish the front hair piece with fabric and trim scraps as desired (E). Pin the front and back hair pieces with right sides together and edges aligned. Stitch along the top edge and around the pointed ends, starting and stopping at placement marks. Clip curves and turn right sides out. Position the hair on the doll's head, and then hand sew it to attach (F).

8 To make the skirt, fold under the bottom edge of the pink patterned fabric and stitch. Run a gathering stitch along the top edge and pull to gather. Pin striped elastic to the gathered edge and stitch (G). Fold the fabric widthwise, right sides together, and stitch. Attach the small pompom to the center back. Hand sew the skirt to the doll (H).

CLOSE AND ALWAYS PRESENT

Ana believes that toys have the power of being "our close and always present best friend." When Ana was growing up, these friends were a softie dog and cow.

A

B

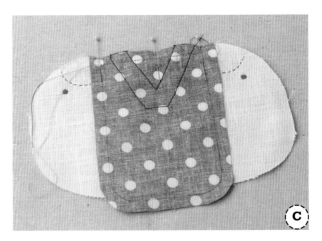

C

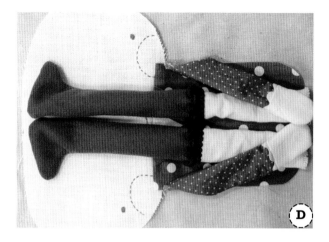

D

G

E

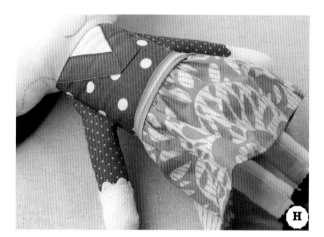

H

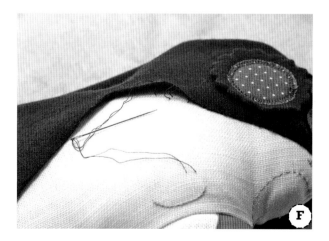

F

POMPOM DOG

Stripes and polka dots make this one jaunty dog. The body is cut and made the same as for Estefania (page 150), but you create your own templates for the head, ears, and shorts.

WHAT YOU'LL NEED

- ✶ Templates (Estefania pages 150–151)
- ✶ Doll Making Tool Kit (page 7)
- ✶ Craft paper and pencil
- ✶ White linen fabric for body, ¼ yard (22.9 cm)
- ✶ Dotted swiss for arms, 8 x 7 inches (20.3 x 17.8 cm)
- ✶ Striped fabric for legs, 4 x 11 inches (10.2 x 27.9 cm)
- ✶ Brown yarn
- ✶ Green print fabric, 4 x 8 inches (10.2 x 20.3 cm)
- ✶ Colorful polka dot fabric, 6 x 8 inches (15.2 x 20.3 cm)
- ✶ Green ribbon, 2 pieces, each 5½ inches (14 cm) long
- ✶ Felt scraps
- ✶ ¼-inch (6 mm) elastic, 4 inches (10.2 cm) long
- ✶ Buttons
- ✶ Pompom

FINISHED SIZE

- ✶ 14 inches (35.6 cm) tall

Before You Begin

For the body front, arms, and legs use the templates from the Estefania doll. Add a ¼ inch (6 mm) seam allowance around the shapes of these and the custom templates before cutting.

For the dog's head, use the craft paper and pencil to make a template that is approximately 8 x 4 inches (20.3 x 10.2 cm). Customize the head to resemble your favorite dog by simply lengthening or shortening the snout. Use the template to cut two pieces from the white linen.

Make a template for the dog's ears that is approximately 1½ x 6 inches (3.8 x 15.2 cm), and use it to cut two pieces each from the linen and the green print.

What You Do

1 Use brown yarn to embroider the mouth and eyes on each side of the dog's face.

2 Align the head pieces with wrong sides together. With the embroidered mouth positioned at the lower left, cut a 2-inch (5.1 cm) slit for the ears at the upper right corner through both layers of fabric (A).

3 With right sides together, pin and stitch the ears. Notch the curves and turn them right side out.

4 Align the two head pieces with right sides together and pin. Slip the ears inside, aligning their raw edges with the slits, and baste. Stitch around the head, leaving an opening at the neck. NOTE: Be careful to keep the ears free of the seam allowance as you sew (B).

5 Open the head, and stitch around the top as shown to sew on the ears (C). Trim the seam allowances, notch at the curves, and turn right side out through the neck opening.

6 Pin the green ribbons to the front body. Measure ¾-inch (1.9 cm) up from the bottom edge and mark the edge of the ribbons with water-soluble marker. Stitch down the sides of both ribbons from the top to this mark, then backstitch to secure Ⓓ. Roll the loose ends of the ribbon away from the bottom edge and pin so they won't get caught later in the seam. Then pin the two back pieces along one of their long edges with right sides together. Leave the opening for stuffing as indicated on the template.

7 With right sides together, pin and stitch the dotted-swiss arms, making sure to leave small openings for stuffing. Fold the striped leg pieces lengthwise, right sides together, pin, and sew, leaving small openings for turning. Clip the curves and turn right sides out Ⓔ.

8 With the front of the doll right side up, position the legs with toes pointing toward the head, raw edges aligned at the bottom. Position the arms with edges aligned at the sides and hands pointing down. Pin and baste. Lay the body back on the front with right sides together, and stitch around the entire outer edge. Trim the seam allowances, clip the curves, and turn right side out through the top opening.

9 Use the polyester fiberfill to stuff the arms and legs, and then whipstitch the openings closed. Stuff the body. Stuff the head and turn the edges of the opening under. Pin the head to the body, and then whipstitch them together, removing pins as you go.

10 Make a basic template for the shorts, and cut one front and one back piece. Use the felt scraps to make pockets on the back Ⓕ. Stitch the front and back together. Fold the top edge down ½ inch (1.3 mm) to make a channel for the elastic. Thread the elastic through the channel, gather, and then sew the ends together.

11 Place the shorts on the dog, and stitch them at the bottom of the suspenders with the buttons Ⓖ. Sew the small pompom to the tip of the dog's snout Ⓗ.

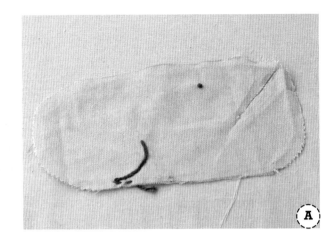

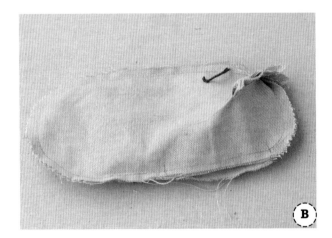

D

G

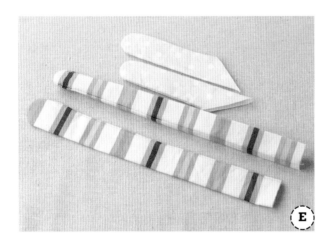

E

H

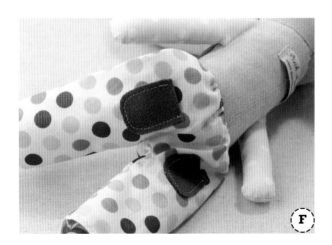

F

CUDDLY EWE

Soft and plushy, this little lamb's a love to hug. Make your own templates for the head, ears, and cape, but use the body template for Estefania (page 150).

WHAT YOU'LL NEED

* Templates (Estefania pages 150–151)
* Doll Making Tool Kit (page 7)
* Craft paper and pencil
* Faux fur fabric, ¼ yard (.23 m)
* Red or pink fabric for arms, 8 x 7 inches (20.3 x 17.8 cm)
* Floral print fabric for legs, 4 x 11 inches (10.2 x 27.9 cm)
* Light brown felt, 10 x 8 inches (25.4 x 20.3 cm)
* Colorful polka dot fabric, 6 x 8 inches (15.2 x 20.3 cm)
* White embroidery floss
* Felt scrap in dark pink
* Polka dot fabric scrap
* Two coordinating fabrics for the cape, 9 x 4½ inches (22.9 x 10.2 cm)
* Dark pink ribbon, ⅝-inch (1.6 mm) wide, 16 inches (40.6 cm) long
* Decorative lace trim, 9 inches (22.9 cm)

FINISHED SIZE

* 16 inches (40.6 cm) tall

Before You Begin

For the body front, back, arms, and legs, use the templates from the Estephania doll. Add a ¼-inch (6 mm) seam allowance around the shapes of these pieces and the custom templates before cutting.

For the lamb's head, use the craft paper and pencil to make a snout template that is approximately 6 x 4 inches (15.2 x 10.2 cm), and a head template that is approximately 3 x 4 inches (7.6 x 10.2 cm). Cut two snouts from the light brown felt, and two head pieces from the faux fur.

Create the lamb's ears by constructing a leaf-shaped template that is approximately 3 x 6 inches (7.6 cm x 15.2 cm) and use it to cut two pieces each from the faux fur and the colorful polka dot fabric.

What You Do

1 Embroider facial features on both sides of the lamb's face using white embroidery floss. Cut two small circles from the felt scraps for the nostrils, and stitch into place. Align each face piece with a head piece, right sides together, and stitch.

2 Align the head pieces with wrong sides together. With the embroidered mouth positioned at the lower left, cut a 2-inch (5.1 cm) slit for the ears at the upper right corner through both layers of fabric (**A**).

3 With right sides together, pin and stitch the ears. Clip the curves and turn them right side out (**B**).

4 Align the two head pieces with right sides together and pin. Slip the ears inside, aligning their raw edges with the slits, and baste (**C**). Stitch around the head, leaving an opening at the neck. Be careful to keep the ears free of the seam allowance as you sew.

5 Open the head, and stitch around the top as for Pompom Dog, step 5 (page 79) to sew in the ears. Trim the seam allowances, notch at the curves, and turn right side out (D).

6 Cut a heart from the dark pink felt and appliqué it to the front of the body (E). Pin the two back pieces along one of their long edges with right sides together. Do not leave an opening in the back since the body will be stuffed from the top opening.

7 With right sides together, pin and stitch the arms, making sure to leave small openings for turning. Fold the leg pieces lengthwise, right sides together, pin, and stitch. Make sure to leave small openings for turning. Notch the curves and turn right side out.

8 With the front of the doll right side up, position the legs with toes pointing toward the head area with their raw edges aligned at the bottom. Position the arms with edges aligned at the sides and hands pointing down. Pin and baste (F). Lay the back of the body on the front with right sides together, and stitch. Trim the seam allowances, notch at the curves, and turn right side out through the back opening.

9 Use the polyester fiberfill to stuff the arms and legs; then stuff the body. Afterwards, stuff the head and turn the edges of the opening under. Pin the head to the body, and then whipstitch them together, removing pins as you go.

10 Make a template for the cape that is approximately 9 x 4½ inches (24.1 x 11.4 cm). Cut one piece from dark pink felt scrap and one piece from polka dot fabric scrap. Lay the fabrics, wrong sides together. Place one edge of decorative lace trim in between these layers and zigzag stitch in place. Fold the ribbon in half lengthwise and place the neckline of the cape in between the fold of the ribbon, then zigzag stitch in place (G).

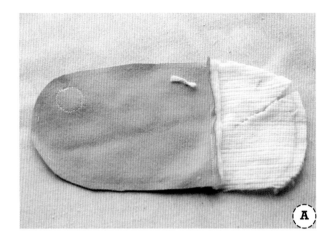

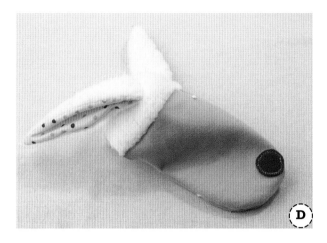

D

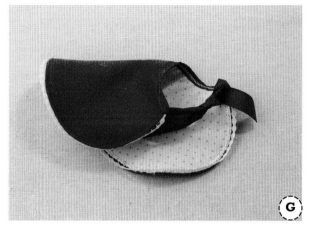

G

E

F

Denise
FERRAGAMO
www.deniseferragamo.com

Denise admits she's under the spell of dolls of all kinds, but especially those that are handmade. "I started making dolls seriously a few years ago, inspired by a book about making cloth dolls which I found in the library. After trying cloth dolls, I experimented with paper clay, gourd, and clay dolls." Denise believes it's the connection between dolls and storytelling that draws many artists to create soft dolls, whether they're novices or advanced sewers. She likes the fact that soft dolls are both versatile and approachable, and that they can be made in any style imaginable.

A Sense of Sharing

Clay still speaks to Denise, and she remains an active member within the pottery community. She also embraces the jewelry, art, and painting communities because she finds the artists are giving and open when it comes to sharing techniques. "I love seeing what others are making and seeing how someone goes about their creative process. It inspires me to take new ideas off in my own direction."

Ritualizing the Process

Creating is not an option for Denise. "Creative people must create as surely as they need to breathe. I couldn't imagine not expressing myself with art. It's an integral part of who I am and what defines me." The finished product is a constant concern for Denise who always fights the need for perfection, which, she admits, can slow her down. She's a big believer in trying new things, but also knows when to stop. "I know what I want to achieve, and will abandon a project if it's not going well. I think it's important to know when to cut your losses and move on if you need to."

Some parts of her process have become so important that Denise finds herself ritualizing them, like her use of turquoise and red. "I love color and don't shy away from using it. I don't think there's a palette I wouldn't try. It all depends on what I'm working on and what mood I'm trying to convey."

Another ritual is the sound of the television on her worktable, which she believes keeps her on task. Since Denise works fulltime outside of doll making, one of her other rituals is going into her studio most evenings as well as spending whole weekends there. Her workroom does quadruple duty. Depending on what she's working on, it's a pottery or paint studio, a print workshop, or a sewing room. Denise is always looking for more space. When her oldest child moved out, she took over the empty room, which, she claims, took about a nanosecond to fill.

Denise believes in sharing her work as well. "When I finish a new piece, I love to share it, even though I'm really a big chicken at heart. I'm always a bit nervous that someone won't like it. But every time I get a positive reaction, I'm a little closer to thinking I might be on the right track." Her interests have led her to using different techniques and materials, including embroidery, appliqué, felt-making, and the use of natural fabrics. "I'm not a great seamstress, so I keep my dolls fairly simple and rely a lot on my embellishment techniques."

FLEUR

With the birds chirping and flowers blooming, demure Fleur is in her element.

WHAT YOU'LL NEED

✴ Templates (pages 152–153)

✴ Doll Making Tool Kit (page 7)

✴ Blue fabric, 2 pieces, one 16 x 10 inches (40.6 x 25.4 cm) for the backing, and one 8 x 8 inches (20.3 x 20.3 cm) for the head front

✴ Green batik fabric for the front body, 16 x 10 inches (40.6 x 25.4 cm)

✴ Flesh-tone felt for the face, 6 x 5 inches (15.2 x 12.7 cm)

✴ Brown or black felt for the hair, 6 x 4 inches (15.2 x 10.2 cm)

✴ Light pink felt, 10 x 3 inches (25.4 x 7.6 cm)

✴ Dark pink felt, 10 x 3 inches (25.4 x 7.6 cm)

✴ Blue felt, 8 x 3 inches (20.3 x 7.6 cm)

✴ Linen, 3 pieces, one 5 x 2 inches (12.7 x 5.1 cm), and two, each 6 x 4 inches (15.2 x 10.2 cm)

✴ Ribbon, 1-inch (2.5 cm) wide, 6 inches (15.2 cm)

✴ Embroidery floss in brown, magenta, and pink

✴ Darning foot

FINISHED SIZE

✴ 14½ inches (36.8 cm) tall

Before You Begin

Cut out all templates and use them to cut the fabrics. Add a ¼-inch (6 mm) seam allowance to the body and head pieces only.

What You Do

1 Pin the head to the front body with both right sides facing up, and then use a ⅛-inch (3 mm) seam allowance to stitch them together. Center the 1-inch (2.5 cm) ribbon over the seam and zigzag along the top and bottom edges to attach (A).

2 With a water-soluble fabric marker, mark the facial features on the flesh-tone felt. Use the stem stitch with brown embroidery floss to embroider the eyes, and the satin stitch with magenta embroidery floss for the mouth. Erase any marks with a damp cloth (B).

3 Attach the pink felt cheeks using the overcast stitch and pink embroidery floss. Pin and stitch the felt hair piece to the face. Sew additional lines of stitching as desired to add interest to the hair.

4 Center, pin, and stitch the embroidered face to the front panel, with the bottom of the face approximately ½ inch (1.3 cm) above the wide ribbon.

5 Appliqué the felt flowers to the body using an overcast stitch, and the leaves using the blanket and running stitches (C).

6 Embroider the word "fleur" on the small linen rectangle and pin it to the front of the body (D). Attach the darning foot to your machine, drop the feed dogs, and use free motion sewing to stitch around the panel several times. Pull away the strands of linen from the edges to create fringe.

7 Pin the body front to the body back, right sides together, and stitch, leaving a 2-inch (5.1 cm) opening on the side for turning (E). Clip and notch the curves. Turn the doll right side out, stuff with the polyester fiberfill, and hand sew to close.

8 Embroider the bird's eyes and wing details onto the right sides of the fabrics. Stitch the wings onto the right sides of the bird body pieces. Pin the bird pieces wrong sides together and stitch, leaving a small opening for stuffing. Do not turn. Stuff with polyester fiberfill, sew the opening closed, and then sew the bird to the top of the doll's head (F).

IMAGINE THAT!

Denise believes her imagination flowered as a child because she spent time with her dolls and other toys. One of her favorites was Chrissie; you pressed a button on her back and her hair grew. Chrissie dressed in cool clothes and looked like the teen Denise wanted to be. "Toys give us an opportunity to sort out our world, and learn how to function in it in a non-threatening way." It's Denise's hope that all kids can have plenty of quality play time every day.

A

B

C

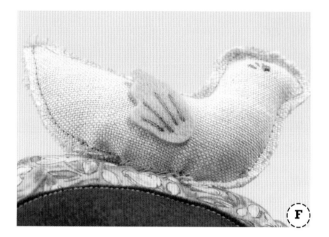

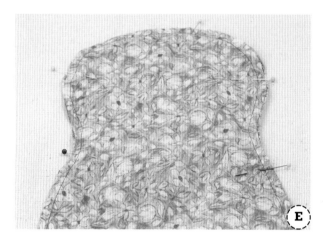

FIRST THINGS FIRST

Denise likes to keep her dolls' faces simple, almost minimalistic. One tip she offers for keeping features aligned is to lay them out on the face, and then mark them with a water-soluble fabric marker. When you've finished sewing them, a quick swipe with a damp cloth makes the marks disappear.

RED MATRYOSHKA

Her bright smile and flower-filled heart make her instantly lovable. Unlike wooden Russian nesting dolls, this Matryoshka returns hugs that are soft and sweet.

WHAT YOU'LL NEED

✳ Templates (pages 154–155)

✳ Doll Making Tool Kit (page 7)

✳ Red fabric for body, 2 pieces, each 15 x 11 inches (38.1 x 27.9 cm)

✳ Pink fabric head front, 7 x 9 inches (17.8 x 22.9 cm)

✳ Flesh-tone felt, 5 x 4 inches (12.7 x 10.2)

✳ Ribbon, ½-inch (1.3 cm) wide, 7 inches (17.8 cm)

✳ Ribbon, ¼-inch (6 mm) wide, 2 pieces, one 8 inches (20.3 cm), one 5 inches (12.7 cm)

✳ Fuchsia felt, 5 x 6 inches (12.7 x 15.2 cm)

✳ White linen, 4 x 5 inches (10.2 x 12.7 cm)

✳ Red felt scraps

✳ Embroidery floss in assorted colors

FINISHED SIZE

✳ 13 inches (33 cm) tall

Before You Begin

Cut out all templates and use them to cut the fabrics. Use pinking shears when cutting the felt heart. Add a ¼-inch (6 mm) seam allowance to the head and body pieces only.

What You Do

1 Pin the head to the body front with both, right sides facing up, and then use a ⅛-inch (3 mm) seam allowance to stitch them together. Center the ½-inch (1.3 cm) ribbon over the seam, and zigzag along the top and bottom edges to attach. Stitch the longer length of ¼-inch (6 mm) ribbon approximately ½ inch (1.3 cm) beneath the first ribbon (A).

2 Use a water-soluble marker to mark the facial features on the flesh-tone felt. Embroider the features using the stem stitch and black floss for the eyes, and the satin stitch with pink and magenta floss for the cheeks and lips (B). Erase any marks with a damp cloth.

CHANGE THE SCENE

When Denise's creative process stalls, she takes herself completely away from the studio and the computer, and goes for a drive or a walk, always with a notebook in hand. The change in scenery provides new perspective and ideas.

3 Center, pin, and stitch the embroidered face to the front panel, with the bottom of the face approximately ½ inch (1.3 cm) above the wider ribbon. Add decorative machine stitching above the wider ribbon, and a running stitch in mint green floss along the bottom edge (C).

4 Pin, and then zigzag stitch the hat to the top of the stitched face. Zigzag stitch the shorter length of ¼-inch (6 mm) ribbon across the bottom edge of the hat. Add decorative embroidery stitches of choice above the ribbon using blue, pink, and magenta embroidery floss.

5 Pin the linen heart on top of the fuchsia felt heart. Use the blanket stitch and red embroidery floss to attach it (D).

6 Cut flower shapes from the red felt scraps and attach them to the heart. Use a variety of embroidery stitches to embellish. Sew the completed heart on the front of the body. Embroider a double running stitch around the stitched heart using pink embroidery floss (E).

7 Pin the body front to the body back, right sides together, and stitch. Clip or notch the curves. Cut a slit approximately 2 inches (5.1 cm) long on the center back of the doll. Use this opening to turn the doll right side out (F). Stuff the doll with the polyester fiberfill and then whipstitch the slit closed.

8 Cut a heart shape from a scrap of red felt. Use the backstitch to embroider the word "love" on it, then sew the heart on the back to cover the stitched opening (G).

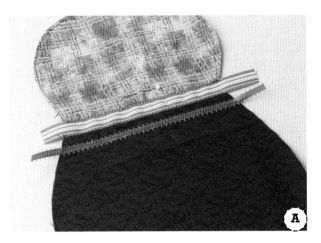

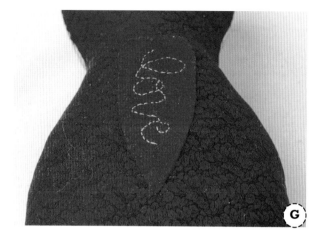

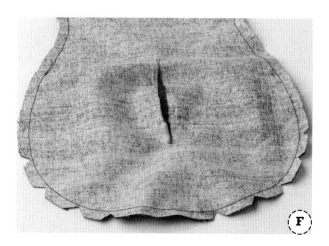

SPRING CLEANING

It all started years ago with a big bag of fabric scraps that Denise's mother sent her after spring cleaning. Since that time, she's filled her stash with recycled thrift-store finds. One of her favorites is the eight yards of designer fabric she bought for three dollars. She also has lots of dyed buttons, ribbons, and lace in bright colors, along with hundreds of embroidery threads. To keep everything easily accessible, she relies on stackable drawer organizers.

Jenn DOCHERTY

www.jenndocherty.com

About seven years ago, a small, pink, slightly malformed, needle-felted teddy bear was born at the creative hands of Jenn Docherty—and everyone loved it! Before that time, friends and followers knew the artist for her jewelry made by traditional wet felting as well as for her delightful fabric handbags. But it was the tiny, imperfect, and thoroughly lovable doll that finally led Jenn to her calling.

Filling in the Blanks

Making dolls for Jenn is about becoming immersed in a miniature world of imaginative play. When she finishes a doll, it literally comes to life for her. "I like to think of my dolls as being born. It's like they wake up with a little character all their own. I think the person who eventually owns the doll will imbibe it with their own story and meaning, which sort of fills in the blanks."

When it comes to process, Jenn feels the end result has to speak to the recipient of the doll as well as its creator. "Sometimes a process comes to define the work. And often, when engaging in a process, your idea grows wings and evolves, going to a place that you never imagined when you started the journey."

Being a dollmaker is certainly something Jenn never imagined. She was not interested in art as a child—except for coloring with her sisters and discovering that you can use nail polish as paint. She imagined growing up to be an archeologist or working in a museum. Studying art history would have made this goal a reality. Instead, Jenn decided to take a textile course and to work for a doll sculptor. Soon, making dolls began to fill in the blanks of Jenn's story.

Slightly Cluttered, Always Creative

Jenn now creates fulltime in her 150-year-old home. The space above her desk is filled with an over abundance of tchotchkes, which she says act as her muses. "An artist's workspace should be slightly cluttered, and filled with tons of great little things to look at and draw inspiration from, sort of like an artist's brain itself."

When Jenn wants to unclutter her brain, she grabs a cup of coffee and plugs in her earphones. "I find that listening to music closes out the outside world and immerses me in the creative moment." Those moments are precious and few since she mostly works while her children are at school or napping. Yet, it's her children who inspire her. She says all of her efforts will have been worth it if, 20 years from now, her daughters become "confident, happy women who have fond memories of growing up in a creative, joyful house."

A Whimsical World

Jenn's needle-felted friends are known for conjuring whimsy. "You can pick them up and engage with them in a way that, for me at least, sparks childhood memories." Her smallest project is a wee penguin, standing about 1½ inches (3.8 cm) tall—proving that whimsy comes in all shapes and sizes.

The colors and textures of her dolls also reflect Jenn's creative perspective. She leans toward using light and cool colors; pale turquoise and mossy greens are favorites. But she enjoys throwing in a dash of pink, and is known for her signature polka dots. "Color can definitely make or break your work. You can have a super cute doll, but if the colors are wrong, it won't succeed. I think it's because color is often the first thing that draws people in. Whether we realize it or not, we all tend to have a visceral reaction to it."

Jenn's book, *Sweet Needle Felts*, has been her biggest project to date, and explores the techniques of creating several of her petite friends. Although she loves wool and has mastered needle felting, Jenn wants to expand her creative horizons through her painting and illustrating. Though she's come a long way from that first pink teddy bear, she still feels there are more characters waiting to be born, stories to bring to life, and hugs to share with a world of whimsical felted friends.

EXPERT TIP

Adding unexpected elements, such as wire or a wooden block, is a terrific way to help create a story for your doll. For example, a doll standing upright can look cute, but a doll standing upright, holding a needle-felted balloon suspended on a piece of wire, helps the doll's personality come alive. We are made to imagine the adventures that the doll has been on, or is about to go on!

BALANCING BUNNY

Who can resist such a well-balanced needle-felted fellow? His smile is your invitation to share his sunny outlook.

WHAT YOU'LL NEED

- Needle felting foam pad
- Felting needle
- Wool stuffing, 3 ounces
- Brown wool roving, 1 ounce
- Brown felt scraps
- White and pink roving scraps
- 2 black glass eyes on wire loops
- Fabric glue
- Embroidery floss and needle
- 3 lengths of nylon beading cord, each 4 inches (10.2 cm)

- Wooden skewer
- Fine-gauge wire
- Wire snips
- Scraps of knit, chambray, and cotton fabric
- Wood disc
- Tacky glue
- Rickrack scrap
- Green wool roving, 1 ounce
- 2 corsage pins, 2 inches (5.2 cm) long
- Yellow and white felt scraps

FINISHED SIZE

- Approximately 6½ inches (16.5 cm) tall

Before You Begin

Due to the sculptural nature of needle felting three-dimensional shapes, you make the doll using your intuitive sense of desired size and proportion. Because sizing may vary doll to doll, there are no templates for clothing and accessories. You will need to draft simple patterns as you go, based on the doll's finished size. To learn how to needle felt, read Needle Felting 1-2-3 on page 103.

What You Do

1 Tightly shape a piece of wool stuffing into a sphere the size of a golf ball. Lay it on the needle felting foam pad. Use the felting needle to felt the ball, turning as you go, until you decrease its size by approximately half (**A**).

2 Wrap a thin layer of the brown roving around the ball, and needle felt until the ball is completely covered (**B**).

3 Cut two, small, elongated triangles from the brown felt scrap as guides for shaping the ears. Wrap a tuft of brown roving around one of the guides and needle felt in place, making sure to keep edges crisp. Leave the bottom fibers loose and unfelted (**C**).

4 Center a small tuft of white roving on the ear and then felt. Create a small pink center by using a smaller tuft of pink. Make the second ear (**D**).

5 Attach the ears to the head by felting the loose fibers at the bottom into the head. Add small tufts of brown roving as needed to strengthen the bond and conceal the join (**E**).

6 Add small tufts of white roving, and then felt them onto the face to create the nose and eyes. Build up the nose with more tufts of wool until it's shaped the way you like it (**F**).

7 Embroider the mouth and nose using brown embroidery floss. Add whiskers by placing a small dab of fabric glue on each of the three pieces of nylon beading cord (G). Insert them into the head at the nose area and pull them through.

8 Form the body by wrapping a large tuft of wool stuffing around a wooden skewer and twirl it between your fingers until the fibers bond to create an egg shape (H). Firmly grasp the tuft and pull it off the skewer. Needle felt the shape until it is firm. Wrap brown wool roving around the shape and felt it in place.

9 Make each of the arms and legs as you did the body by wrapping the roving on the skewer and shaping each into a tiny oblong. After needle felting, when the shapes are firm, needle felt brown roving around each limb.

10 Position the legs, and needle felt them in place as you did for attaching the ears. Use tufts of brown roving to strengthen the joins and to create a nice seamless shape.

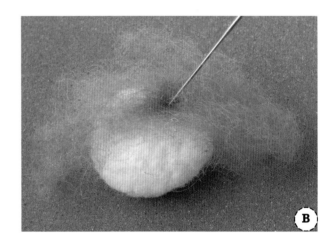

11 To fashion the shirt, wrap a scrap of knit fabric around the body with right sides together. Trim the fabric to fit lengthwise and widthwise including a small seam allowance at the back. Stitch to create a tube, then turn right side out. Slip the tube on the bunny's torso. Stitch a running stitch along the top edge, pull to gather, and tie off.

12 Construct each sleeve using the same technique as in step 11. Thread a needle with the tails of the gathering thread and stitch back and forth to ensure that the arms are fully attached to each sleeve (I). Stitch the arms to the body.

13 To attach the head, thread the fine-gauge wire onto the doll needle. Insert the needle up through the doll's bottom, out through the neck, in through the bottom of the head, and out the top. Turn the needle and go back the way you came (J). Pull tightly, twist the wire to secure, and use the snips to trim off any excess. Needle felt small tufts of wool to cover the dents in the head and bottom.

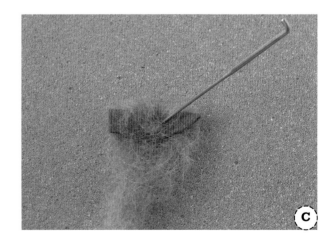

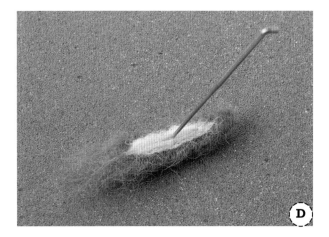

D

G

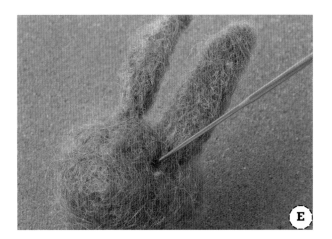

E

H

F

I

14 To make the trousers, wrap a scrap of chambray fabric around the body, below the shirt. Trim to fit the body's circumference, mark the seam line, and be sure to add a seam allowance at the top (waist) and bottom (legs) for hemming.

15 Hem the top and bottom edges. Align the short ends, right sides together, and stitch to make a tube (**K**). With the tube inside out, slip it on the bunny to check the fit. Stitch a few hand stitches between the bunny's legs to shape the legs and tie off. Turn the shorts right side out. Felt a small white ball for the bunny's tail and stitch or glue to the back of the trousers.

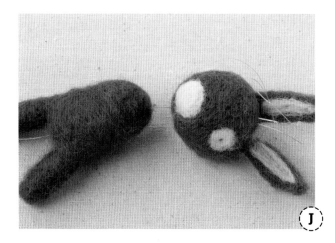

16 Make the base. Cut a 3-inch (7.6 cm) circle from cotton fabric. Center the wood disc on the circle and use the tacky glue to glue it in place. Clip around the circle at ¼-inch (6 mm) intervals, then glue the fabric to the sides of the disc. Glue a felt circle to the bottom of the disc, and then glue the rickrack around the sides. Allow the glue to dry.

17 Needle felt a ping-pong-size ball from green wool roving. On the bottom of the green felted ball, needle felt two indentations to accommodate the pearl heads of the corsage pins. Poke the pins up through the green ball and place dabs of fabric glue onto the points (**L**). Insert the pins into the bunny's legs, and allow the glue to dry before gluing the ball to the base.

18 Cut yellow and white felt scraps for the flower. Needle felt a tuft of green wool roving to the center. Glue the 18-gauge wire to the back of the flower for the stem. Use the doll needle to poke a hole in the bunny's hand. Apply glue to the wire, insert it into the hole, and allow the glue to dry.

NEEDLE FELTING 1-2-3

Needle felting is a way to get the same textural feel of felted fabric without going through the washing and drying process. You can needle felt layers onto other fabrics, or create three-dimensional shapes. The tools and materials are readily available through many online sources. The following general instructions are for felting three-dimensional shapes for making dolls.

Wool Roving

To needle felt, you use a special needle to repeatedly jab wool roving into other fabric (when you're layering), or into itself or wool stuffing or batting (when you're making three-dimensional shapes). Roving is wool before it's been spun and twisted into lengths of yarn. It's soft and fluffy, having

been combed and loosely twisted so the fibers minimally hold together. You can purchase wool roving that's already dyed, or you can try dyeing it yourself. Wool stuffing is the same as polyester fiberfill, except made from wool, and wool batting is the traditional on-a-roll filling for quilts.

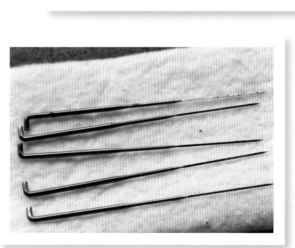

Needles and Foam Pad

The felting needle has barbs on the end which push the roving into the fabric or wool stuffing, and, at the same time, help the fibers bond to one another. Because you'll be using firm repetitive motions when needle felting, you'll need a special, 2-inch-thick (5.1 cm) foam pad. It prevents the needle from damaging your work surface—not to mention preventing you from stabbing your fingers!

Shapes, Colors, and Facial Features

To begin, place your piece of foam pad onto a sturdy worktable. The foam needs to be large enough for you to comfortably needle felt the pieces for the doll. Pull off a piece of wool stuffing or batting and roll it into a loose ball. Lay it on the foam pad, then use the needle to quickly jab in and out of the ball until you reduce it to the size you want. As you work, you can also shape the piece to elongate it or make it more ovular or cylindrical. When you're finished, it will feel firm, fuzzy, and felted. To add color, needle felt colored roving into the base piece.

When you're making a doll, you felt the pieces for the limbs or ears separately, then use the same technique to attach them. For three-dimensional facial features, such as noses, eyelids, chins, and cheeks, add pieces of roving and sculpt them as desired. If you want a flat feature, such as a circle for an eye, use the needle-felting technique to layer a piece of roving onto the shape.

CHICKIE IN A KERCHIEF

Though she has tiny yellow wings, this little chickie prefers to walk to the market so she can show off her cute kerchief.

WHAT YOU'LL NEED

* Needle felting foam pad
* Felting needle
* Wool stuffing, 3 ounces
* Pale yellow wool roving, 1 ounce
* Wooden skewer
* Black upholstery thread and needle
* 2 black felt scraps
* Cosmetic blush
* Cotton swab
* Fine-gauge wire
* 5-inch (12.7 cm) doll needle

* Yellow felt scraps
* 2 small red buttons
* 2 lengths of 18-gauge black craft wire, each 2 inches (7.6 cm)
* Wire snips
* Fabric glue
* Print fabric scraps
* Embroidery floss and needle
* Craft drill
* Toy wooden block
* Tacky glue

FINISHED SIZE

* Approximately 5½ inches (14 cm) tall

Before You Begin

Due to the sculptural nature of needle felting three-dimensional shapes, you make the doll using your intuitive sense of desired size and proportion. Because sizing may vary doll to doll, there are no templates for clothing and accessories. To learn how to needle felt, read Needle Felting 1-2-3 on page 103.

What You Do

1 Tightly shape a piece of wool stuffing into a sphere the size of a golf ball. Lay it on the needle felting foam pad. Use the felting needle to felt the ball, turning as you go, until you decrease its size by approximately half (A).

2 Wrap a thin layer of the pale yellow roving around the ball and needle felt until the ball is completely covered.

3 Form the body by wrapping a large tuft of wool stuffing around the wooden skewer; twirl it between your fingers until the fibers bond to create a thick cylinder. Firmly grasp the tuft and pull it off the skewer. Needle felt until firm. Wrap pale yellow roving around the shape and felt it in place.

4 Make and attach the tail by folding a tuft of pale yellow roving in half. Felt on the folded end until it is a firm U-shape, leaving loose fibers at the other end (B). Attach the loose ends to the bottom of the body and felt until firmly attached, adding more roving as needed to build up and smooth out the shape.

5 Thread a black seed bead on a length of the upholstery thread, then insert both ends of the thread into the eye of the doll needle. At the desired position for one of the eyes, insert the needle, bring it out at the base of the head, and tie off. Repeat for the other eye.

Fold the black wool felt scrap in half, and cut out a long oval for the beak. Fold it in half to form the upper and lower beaks. Position the felt on the head, and needle felt it at the center to attach (C). Use the upholstery thread to embroider tiny stitches for the eyebrows above each eye. Apply a small amount of cosmetic blush with a cotton swab for the rosy cheeks.

7 Attach the head to the body. Thread fine-gauge wire onto the doll needle. Insert the needle up through the doll's bottom, out through the neck, in through the bottom of the head, and out the top. Turn the needle and go back the way you came (D). Pull tightly, twist the wire to secure, and then use the wire snips to trim off any excess. Needle felt small tufts of wool to cover the dents in the head and bottom.

8 Make a template for the wings and use it to cut them out of the yellow felt. Stitch the wings to the body using the small buttons.

9 Use the doll needle to make two holes at the bottom of the body. Put a dab of fabric glue on one end of each piece of black craft wire. Insert the wires into the holes, and allow to dry (E).

10 To make the dress, cut a length of fabric to fit your doll. Fold in half lengthwise, right sides together, stitch the long edge, and turn right side out. Fold in the raw edges on the short sides and press. Topstitch around the piece, leaving a channel open across the top edge. Thread a length of embroidery floss through the channel (F). Pull to gather and tie tightly around the chick just under the wings.

11 Cut two matching triangles for the kerchief and stitch on all sides, leaving an opening for turning. Turn right side out, fold in the raw edges, and stitch to close. Stitch a length of embroidery thread along the long side of the triangle and use it to tie the kerchief to the head (G).

12 Use the craft drill to make holes in the toy wooden block to accommodate the leg wires. Place a dab of tacky glue in each hole, insert the legs, and allow to dry.

A

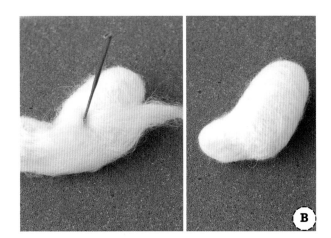

B

C

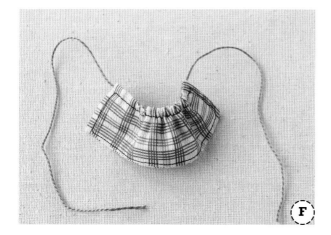

POPPY THE PIG

Poppy is proof you can dress up a pig and take her to town. Needle felting makes it easy for you to sculpt her features—including her cute curly tail.

WHAT YOU'LL NEED

- Needle felting foam pad
- Felting needle
- Wool stuffing, 3 ounces
- Pale peach wool roving, 1 ounce
- Black upholstery thread and needle
- 2 black seed beads
- Cosmetic blush
- Cotton swab
- Wooden skewer
- Fine-gauge wire
- 5-inch (12.7 cm) doll needle
- Wire snips
- Cotton print fabric scraps
- Rickrack scraps
- Fabric glue
- 2 ½-inch (6.4 cm) wood disc
- Tacky glue
- Yellow felt scraps
- Pinking shears
- Two straight pins
- Aqua wool roving scraps
- Ribbon, 6 inches (15.2 cm)
- 1 length of 18-gauge wire, 5 inches (12.7 cm) long
- Awl

FINISHED SIZE

- Approximately 6 inches (15.2 cm) tall

Before You Begin

Due to the sculptural nature of needle felting three-dimensional shapes, you make the doll using your intuitive sense of desired size and proportion. Because sizing may vary doll to doll, there are no templates for clothing and accessories. To learn how to needle felt, read Needle Felting 1-2-3 on page 103.

What You Do

1 Tightly shape a piece of wool stuffing into a sphere the size of a golf ball. Lay it on the needle felting foam pad. Use the felting needle to felt the ball, turning as you go, until you decrease its size by approximately half.

2 Wrap a thin layer of the pale peach roving around the ball and needle felt until the ball is completely covered.

3 Make the ears by rolling two equally sized tufts of pale peach roving into small balls. Gently needle felt one ball until it starts to firm up. Then, start felting in the middle of the ball to make the crook of the ear. Finally, taper one side to make the tip.

4 Position the ear on the head and attach it by felting through the base of the ear. Add small tufts of pink roving as needed to strengthen the bond and conceal the join (A). Repeat for the other ear.

5 To make the snout, start with a small, loosely felted ball of pale peach roving. Attach it to the center of the face, and felt. Add small tufts of pink roving as needed to strengthen the bond and conceal the join. Make small indentations for each nostril by jabbing the needle into the same spot several times (B).

6 Thread a black seed bead on a length of the upholstery thread, then insert both ends through the eye of the doll needle. At the desired position for one of the eyes, insert the needle, bring it out at the base of the head, and tie off. Repeat for the other eye. Apply a small amount of cosmetic blush with a cotton swab for the rosy cheeks.

7 To construct the body, wrap a large tuft of wool stuffing around the wooden skewer and twirl it between your fingers until the fibers bond to create a thick cylinder. Firmly grasp the tuft and pull it off the skewer. Needle felt until firm. Wrap pale peach roving around the shape and felt it in place.

8 Make each of the arms and legs as you did the body by wrapping the roving on the skewer and shaping each into an elongated oblong. Completely felt the arms with peach roving. For the legs, leave one end on each un-felted. Attach the legs to the body at their un-felted ends. Add small tufts of pink roving as needed to strengthen the bond and conceal the joins.

9 Form the tail by wrapping a small tuft of wool stuffing around a 3-inch (7.6 cm) length of the fine-gauge wire. Twist with your fingers until the fibers bond to make a 1-inch (2.5 cm) snake. Slip the tail off the wire, felt until firm, and then gently felt it to the back of the body. Add small tufts of pink roving as needed to strengthen the bond and conceal the join (C).

10 Affix the head to the body. Thread fine-gauge wire onto the doll needle. Insert the needle up through the doll's bottom, out through the neck, up through the bottom of the head and out the top. Turn the needle and go back the way you came (D). Pull tightly, twist the wire to secure, and then use the wire snips to snip off any excess. Needle felt small tufts of wool to cover the dents in the head and bottom.

11 Create the dress by cutting a length of fabric to fit your doll. Fold in half lengthwise, right sides together, stitch the long edge, and turn right side out. Fold in the raw edges on the short sides and press. Topstitch around the piece, leaving a channel open across the top edge (E). Thread a length of embroidery floss through the channel. Wrap the dress around the pig, pull to gather, and tie off tightly at the back of the neck. Use the fabric glue to attach the rickrack around the hem.

12 To attach the arms, begin by threading the doll needle with upholstery thread to make an unknotted double strand. Insert the needle through the top of one arm. Leave the tails inside, exit at the armpit, and make a knot. Run the needle and thread through the upper body, over the dress, and tie a knot. Stitch on the other arm (see Rotating Joints, page 9). Run the needle through the body, exiting at the bottom of the body and tie off.

13 Form the base. Cut a 3-inch (7.6 cm) circle from cotton fabric. Center the wood disc on the circle and use the tacky glue to glue it in place. Clip around the circle at ¼-inch (6 mm) intervals, then glue the fabric to the sides of the disk. Glue a felt circle to the bottom of the disk, and glue the rickrack around the sides. Allow the glue to dry.

14 Construct the small felt cushion by using pinking shears to cut two 2-inch (5.1 cm) circles from the yellow felt. Stitch around, leaving a small opening, stuff with wool stuffing, and stitch closed (F).

15 Poke the pins up through cushion. Place dabs of fabric glue onto the points. Insert the pins into the pig's legs. Allow the glue to dry before using tacky glue to glue the doll to the base.

16 Needle felt a balloon from the aqua roving. Run a thread through a length of mini rickrack, and pull to gather to create a small rosette. Glue the rosette to the bottom of the balloon. Use the doll needle to make a hole in the bottom of the balloon, and glue one end of the 18-guage wire in it.

17 With the awl, poke a hole through the hand, then pull the wire through it. Allow it to rest on the felt base, using a small dab of tacky glue to adhere it. Make a bow from the ribbon and glue it to the head.

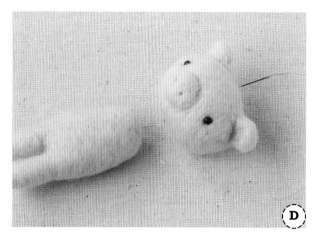

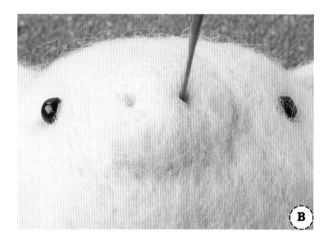

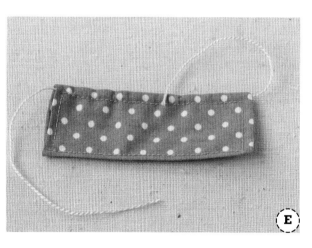

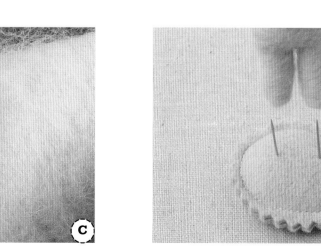

Suse BAUER

www.revoluzza.com

Very few people know that Suse Bauer doesn't really enjoy sewing—she just likes what happens when she does. In fact, if Suse had her way, she'd be learning to knit and crochet. She studied fine art in college, a background that comes in handy when sketching her doll ideas, and is still active in the illustration community. "I couldn't sew or use a sewing machine when I started," says Suse. "They were skills I had to learn, and now I use them every day."

Eco-Friends

When Suse had children, she began cooking organic food and bought eco-friendly clothing made without chemical dyes. When her daughter was born, she looked for special dolls to buy, but didn't find any she liked or that weren't full of chemicals. In the process, she learned that many toys were chemically polluted and produced under bad conditions, some including the use of child labor.

So Suse bought a cheap sewing machine and set out to make the perfect toy herself—and it changed her life forever. She believes each doll has a unique story that's not revealed during the process, but only becomes known when it's done. "The moment a doll is finished and her story is written, I focus on making the next one, and I'm more than willing to give away the finished one."

Share and Share Alike

Suse shares her love of doll making by offering free tutorials and patterns for her projects. This controversial approach proves how dedicated she is to spreading the word about dolls and encouraging others to sew. She has had to face the criticism that nobody would buy her dolls if she offered free patterns. But Suse disagrees. The response to her approach, from all over the world, has been amazing. "It's so wonderful and inspiring to see the different interpretations of my dolls, especially when you look at the different cultural backgrounds of the makers," says Suse.

As a former a multimedia designer, she believes there is no need to keep secrets, and has always been fond of open content sites like

Wikipedia. Show and tell is "the beginning of a creative process" for her and other dollmakers alike. She receives pictures of many finished projects based on her patterns because dollmakers upload images onto Suse's Flickr group for their own show and tell. She even admits to learning a thing or two from the people using her patterns.

Losing Sleep over Dolls

Even though she was "never drawn to dolls much as a child," Suse remembers two Käthe Kruse dolls she liked, though she likes them even more today. As a kid, their hand-painted faces and human hair freaked her out. Scarier still, she remembers a doll at her aunt's house that gave her bad dreams. One day she destroyed the doll's face and buried it. Later Suse learned that this doll was a childhood favorite of her aunt's which she had during World War II. Though the nightmares ended for Suse, her aunt remained pretty angry over the doll's destruction.

Today, her once rocky relationship with dolls has now turned into a full-blown labor of love. She likes to get to work very early, starting before her family wakes up, and continues working late into the night. When she's really in the zone, she'll work until 3 a.m., sleep for three hours, then wake to continue her project. And her hard work, which combines handcrafting and art, always yields special results, whether she's sewing tiny monsters to cheer up her daughter,

or sewing 66 monsters from a Paul Klee painting for the German National Gallery. In the future, Suse hopes to produce a line of fair trade, chemical-free toys. And, if her past creative history is any indication, it's a goal she will achieve.

RED RIDING HOOD

Red's cherry cheeks and sweet smile cover up her secret weapon. Her lovely long legs make it easy to run away from any big bad wolf.

WHAT YOU'LL NEED

✳ Templates (pages 156–157)

✳ Doll Making Tool Kit (page 7)

✳ Scrap felt pieces for the face, hair, cheeks, and collar

✳ Red polka dot fabric, 8 x 16 inches (20.3 x 40.6 cm)

✳ Print fabric for the body, 8 x 16 inches (20.3 x 40.6 cm)

✳ White linen, 6 x 6 inches (15.2 x 15.2 cm)

✳ Red striped fabric, 5 x 7 inches (12.7 x 17.8 cm)

✳ Scrap fabric for shoes

✳ Embroidery floss, red and pink

✳ Embroidery needle

✳ 1 button

FINISHED SIZE

✳ 17 inches (43.2 cm) tall

Before You Begin

Cut out all templates along the solid lines. When you cut the fabric, add a ¼-inch (6 mm) seam allowance around each shape, except for the felt appliqué pieces (face, hair, cheeks, and collar). Transfer all markings to the wrong side of the fabric.

What You Do

1 Pin the felt appliqué pieces for the face, hair, and cheeks onto a red hood piece Ⓐ. Machine stitch all pieces in place. Embroider the eyes, nose, mouth, freckles, and hairpin details with the pink and red embroidery floss and needle Ⓑ.

2 Pin and stitch the top edge of the front body piece to the bottom edge of the red hood, with right sides together. Repeat for the back side. Stitch the appliqué collar to the front of the neck Ⓒ. Sew the button onto the collar.

STROLLING FOR INSPIRATION

For Suse, it's always a good time for a walk. It doesn't matter to her if it's late at night or early morning. Whether she's walking in Berlin or through the forest, Suse claims a good stroll clears her head and opens her up to new ideas.

3 With right sides together, pin and stitch the white linen arm pieces to the sleeve ends on the front and back body pieces (**D**).

4 Pin and stitch the shoes to the legs with right sides together (**E**). Then, with right sides together, pin and stitch the legs, leaving the top open for turning. Clip the curves. Turn the legs right side out, and stuff with the polyester fiberfill (**F**).

5 Place the front of the doll on top of the back of the doll with right sides together. Align all edges, and stitch all the way around, except for the bottom edge and the side opening (**G**).

6 Slip the legs in between the stitched layers from the bottom edge. Align the raw edges, with the feet pointing toward the head, and pin. Stitch the bottom edge carefully, removing the pins as you go. Trim the seam allowances, clip the curves, and turn the entire doll right side out through the side opening.

7 Stuff the arms with polyester fiberfill through the opening. To keep the stuffing in the arms, stitch a seam across the top of the arm from shoulder to armpit.

8 Stuff the rest of the doll with polyester fiberfill through the opening and whipstitch the opening closed.

HAIR LOSS

As a child, Suse had one special toy, a little plush dog. She loved it so much that the poor pup had to be washed a million times in the washing machine. In this quest for cleanliness, the pup lost almost all of his hair and one of his ears.

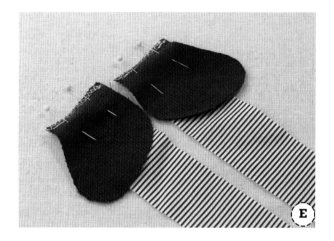

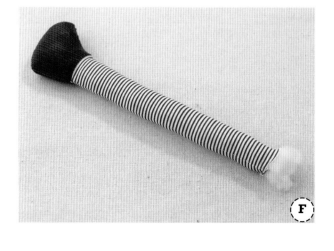

Katie
SHELTON
www.skunkboycreatures.com

Looking at Katie Shelton's creatures gives you an insight to her sunny disposition and doll-making philosophy. "When has a doll ever made someone sad? They're little smile makers." Katie claims she was once uncreative. "I used to feel like I didn't have a talent and wasn't good at anything. I didn't feel naturally creative like most artsy folk, and I had no idea how to express myself in that way." But that all changed when Katie began making dolls. Now she takes pride in delighting us with her parade of whimsical creatures.

Losing Her Head

After the birth of Katie's first child, she decided to try her hand at sewing a toy for her daughter. One finished animal led to another—then came the local art shows and handmade boutiques. Etsy soon followed, and even more orders flooded in. Suddenly, Katie was creating more than she ever thought she could.

Many of her orders are custom requests. Katie points out that these dolls have stories before they're ever created. But custom made or not, Katie believes they each have their own story sewn into them.

Katie's own memorable tales of doll making involve an insect and a dinosaur. Katie recently made a bee brooch for a special cause, which became the tiniest softie she's ever made. And once, Katie had to produce a T-Rex on a tight deadline. While trying to perfect the pattern, Katie ended up with seven dinosaur heads on the table. When her husband walked in, he saw the heads, then saw Katie with her head in her hands, and he wondered if she had truly lost her own head over the project.

Katie's run-in with the T-Rex shows her intense focus on whatever product she's creating. "If the end goal is a beautiful product, then I am definitely guilty of focusing on that! I do agree that the process is important, but nothing makes me happier than finishing something that makes me feel really satisfied."

EXPERT TIP

Felt is one of my favorite materials to use when making dolls. Rather than using ordinary craft felt, I recommend splurging on either wool felt or bamboo felt. These quality materials help dolls look their very best.

Nailing It

When it comes to process, Katie does her work among heaping piles of fabric and felt. "I'm a terribly unorganized person," says Katie, who doesn't have specific sewing hours. One important ingredient for working is playing movies or music in the background. Katie says the noise helps distract her from the more redundant and tedious parts of doll making.

Repetition does have its rewards though. Katie prides herself on estimating proportions. She says she can nail the sizing on the first try. Katie is also especially productive when setting little goals. When she reaches a goal, she celebrates with a prize that can be anything from a special snack to 30 minutes of online shopping.

It's hard to believe Katie was once shy with colors, when you see the many patterns and palettes on her plushies today. "I used to be afraid of using vibrant colors," she admits. Luckily, Katie's custom orders motivated her to stretch her imagination beyond her beloved black and white. Now, she exclaims, "Cheery and colorful are equally great!"

As far as the future is concerned, Katie's mindset is definitely goal-oriented. For a once self-described uncreative person, she has blossomed into a prodigious artist for whom anything is possible. Katie is eager to learn quilting and promises, "I'll be a quilter one day, and I'll make the most beautiful quilts to display all over my house and give to all my friends and family."

LOVELY LITTLE LAMB

This dainty creature has a fleece made of creamy yellow felt—the kind even Mary's little lamb would envy.

WHAT YOU'LL NEED

* Template (page 158)
* Doll Making Tool Kit (page 7)
* Gray wool felt, ¼ yard (22.9 cm)
* Pink wool felt scrap
* Pale yellow wool felt, ¼ yard (22.9 cm)
* Perle cotton
* 2 buttons
* Fabric glue
* Pink embroidery floss and needle

FINISHED SIZE

* 8 inches (20.3 cm) tall

Before You Begin

Cut out the templates along the solid lines. There is no seam allowance involved with these templates because all pieces are sewn together with an overcast stitch.

What You Do

1 Use perle cotton with the overcast stitch to sew the front and back of the body together. Leave an opening at the neck for stuffing. Stuff the body with polyester fiberfill, and stitch the opening closed.

2 Sew the front and back of the head together with perle cotton and the overcast stitch (A). Leave an opening at the neck for stuffing. Stuff the head with polyester fiberfill, and stitch the opening closed.

THE JOY OF SEWING

"I don't advise working when you aren't inspired," says Katie. "Sewing when you're uninspired takes the joy out of it, and that's sort of the whole point. Plus, your work will suffer for it." Katie also recommends taking a break now and then to help you find whatever you need to bring the inspiration back. "Don't worry. That sewing project will still be waiting for you when you return."

3 Attach the buttons for the eyes using the perle cotton. Use the fabric glue to attach small circles of the pink felt for the cheeks. Embroider a nose with the satin stitch using the pink embroidery floss (**B**). Sew the head to the body.

4 With the perle cotton, make long straight stitches to attach the cut circles of pale yellow felt to the body only (not the face). Completely cover the gray felt by alternating large, medium, and small circles to fill the entire area (**C**).

5 Pinch the ears in half and sew onto either side of the head (**D**). Pinch the tail in half and hand stitch to the body.

MR. STRONG

Body

Cut 2 from flesh-tone fabric

Upper Body Backing

Cut 1 of the upper portion of this oval from white felt

Open

★ Placement guides for facial
 features are in gray. Do not
 cut these face parts.

★ These pieces are shown at
 full size and do not need to
 be enlarged.

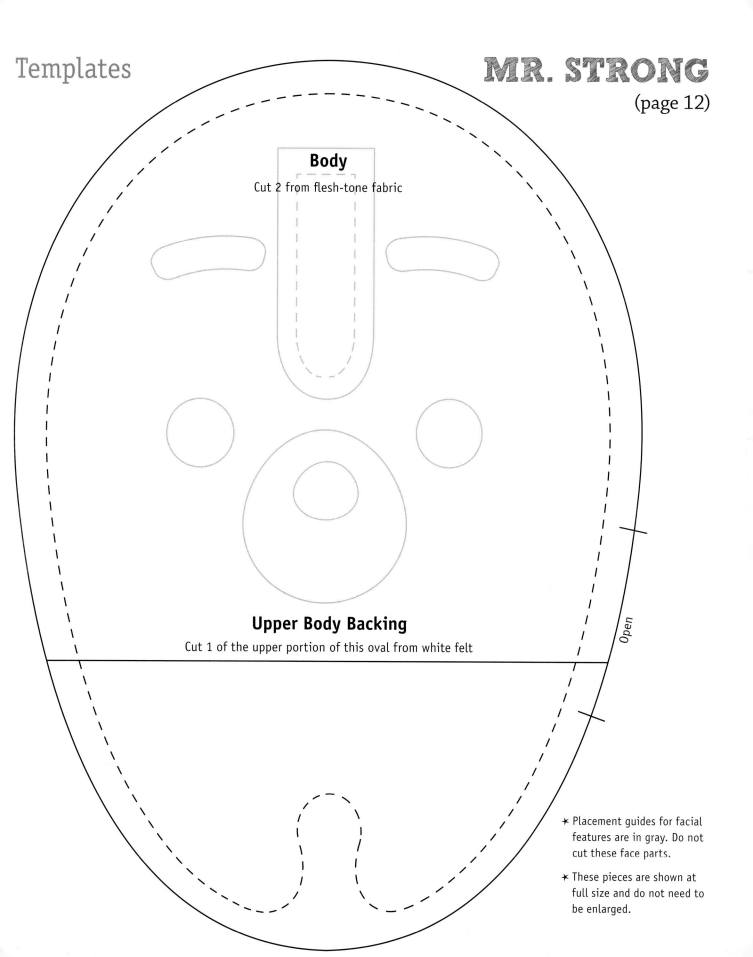

MR. STRONG

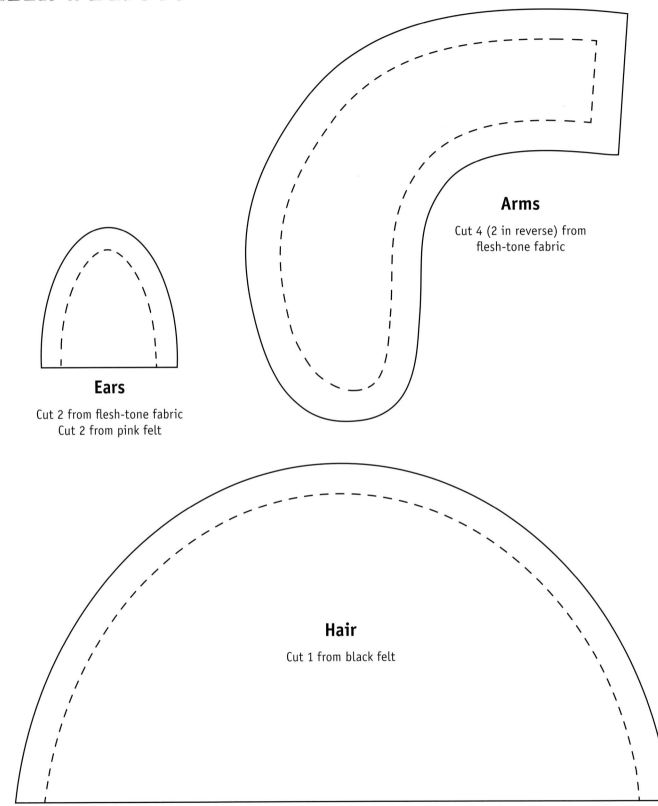

Arms

Cut 4 (2 in reverse) from
flesh-tone fabric

Ears

Cut 2 from flesh-tone fabric
Cut 2 from pink felt

Hair

Cut 1 from black felt

MR. STRONG

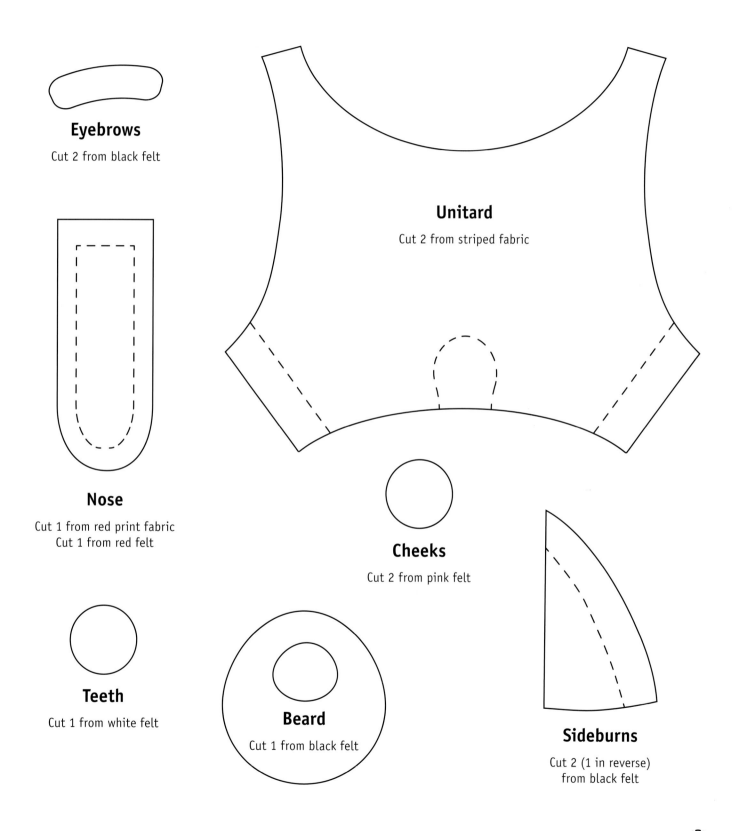

Eyebrows

Cut 2 from black felt

Unitard

Cut 2 from striped fabric

Nose

Cut 1 from red print fabric
Cut 1 from red felt

Cheeks

Cut 2 from pink felt

Teeth

Cut 1 from white felt

Beard

Cut 1 from black felt

Sideburns

Cut 2 (1 in reverse)
from black felt

MR. GRUMPY

(page 16)

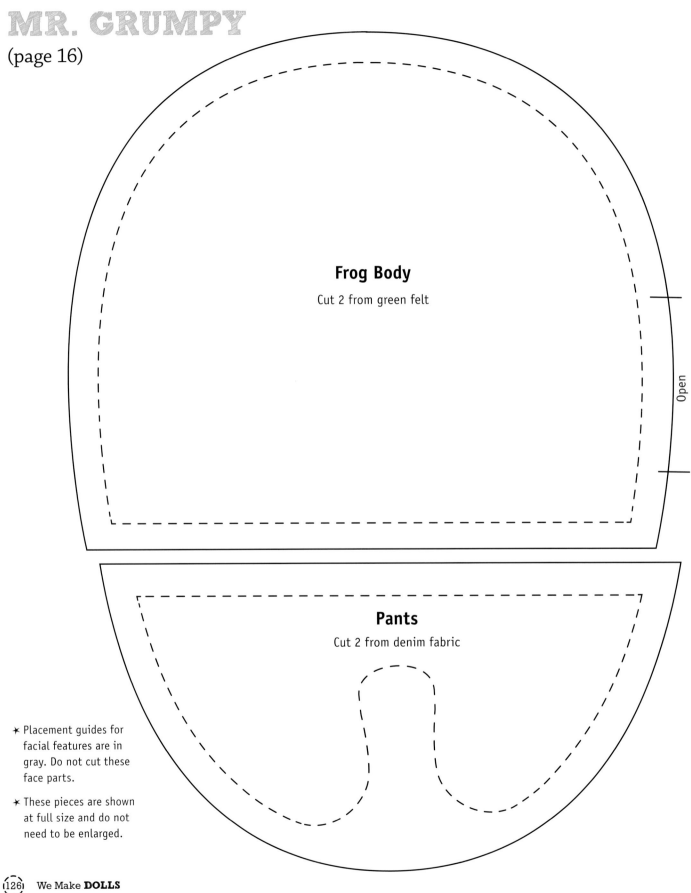

Frog Body

Cut 2 from green felt

Open

Pants

Cut 2 from denim fabric

★ Placement guides for facial features are in gray. Do not cut these face parts.

★ These pieces are shown at full size and do not need to be enlarged.

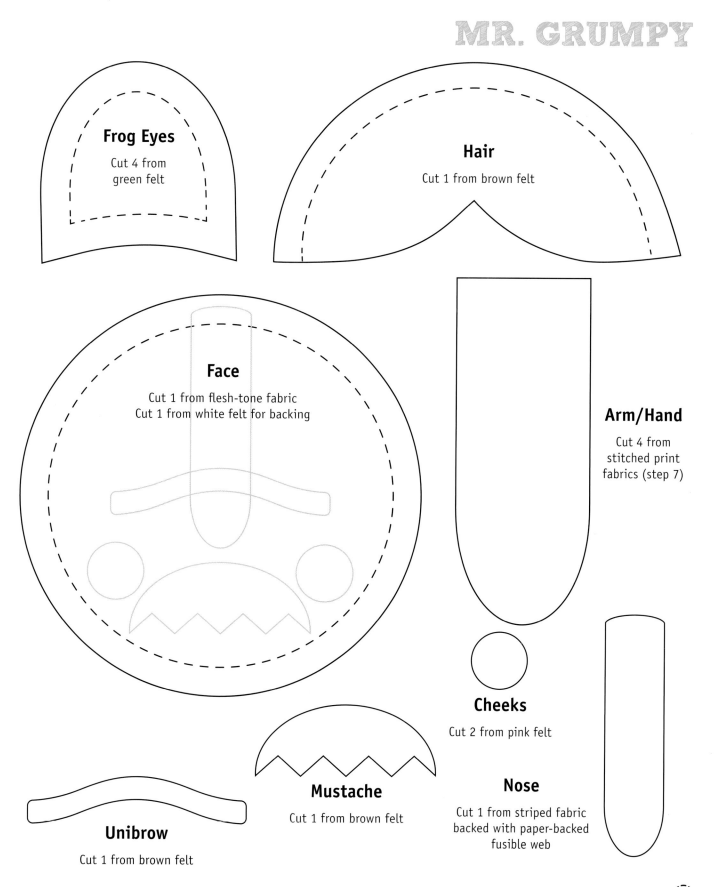

Frog Eyes

Cut 4 from green felt

Hair

Cut 1 from brown felt

Face

Cut 1 from flesh-tone fabric
Cut 1 from white felt for backing

Arm/Hand

Cut 4 from stitched print fabrics (step 7)

Cheeks

Cut 2 from pink felt

Nose

Cut 1 from striped fabric backed with paper-backed fusible web

Mustache

Cut 1 from brown felt

Unibrow

Cut 1 from brown felt

SUPER GIRL

(page 20)

★ Placement guides for facial features are in gray. Do not cut these face parts.

★ These pieces are shown at full size and do not need to be enlarged.

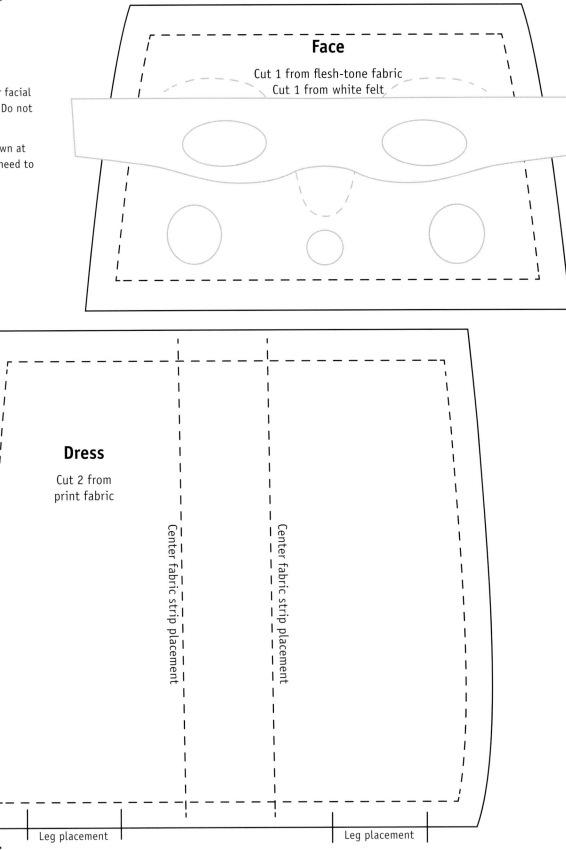

Face

Cut 1 from flesh-tone fabric
Cut 1 from white felt

Dress

Cut 2 from print fabric

Center fabric strip placement

Center fabric strip placement

Leg placement

Leg placement

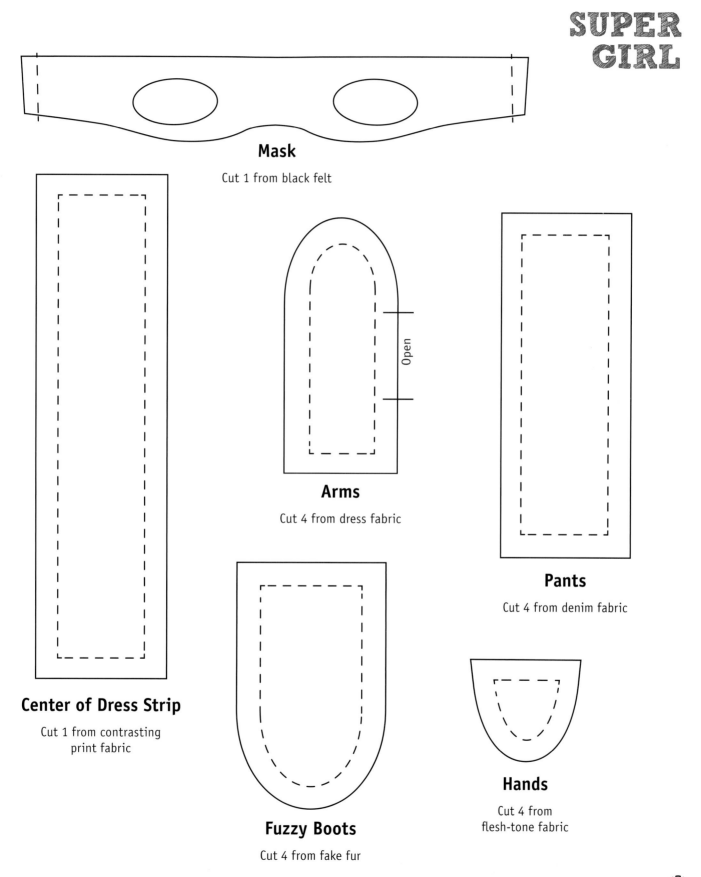

SUPER GIRL

Mask

Cut 1 from black felt

Arms

Cut 4 from dress fabric

Open

Pants

Cut 4 from denim fabric

Center of Dress Strip

Cut 1 from contrasting
print fabric

Fuzzy Boots

Cut 4 from fake fur

Hands

Cut 4 from
flesh-tone fabric

SUPER GIRL

Cheeks

Cut 2 from
pink felt

Lips

Cut 1 from
red felt

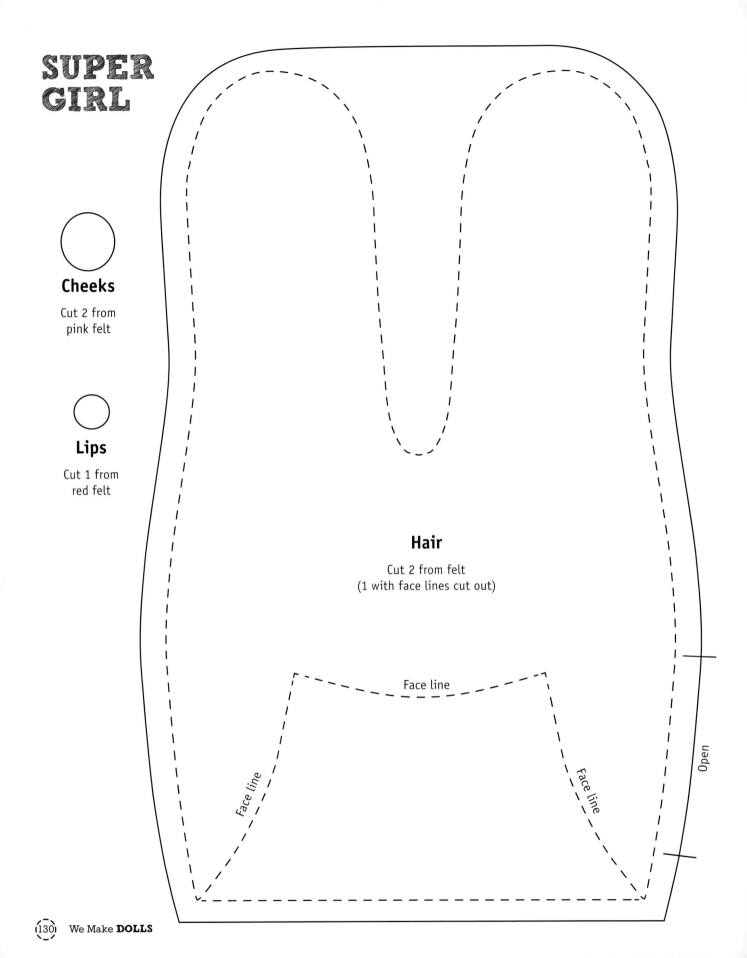

Hair

Cut 2 from felt
(1 with face lines cut out)

Face line

Face line

Face line

Open

MERRY MERMAID

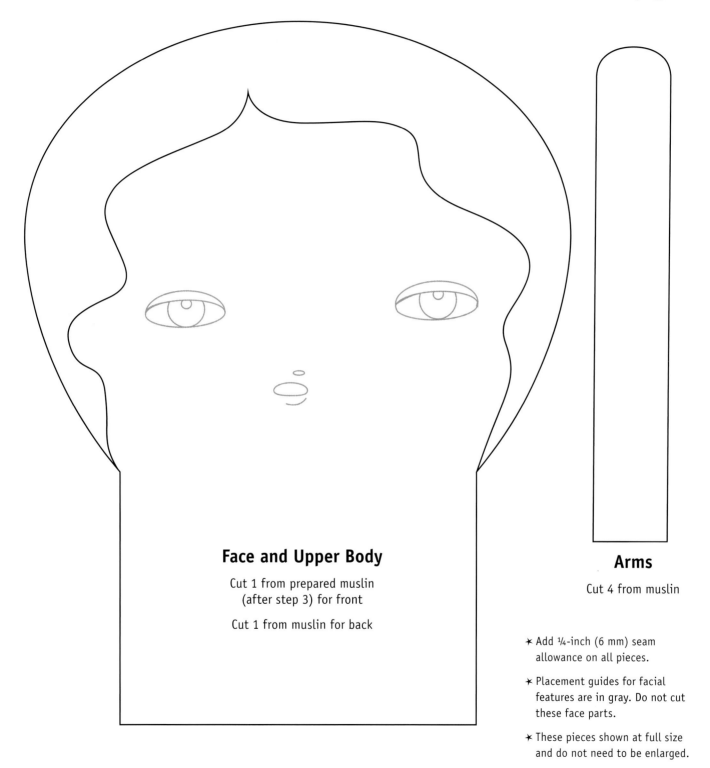

Face and Upper Body

Cut 1 from prepared muslin
(after step 3) for front

Cut 1 from muslin for back

Arms

Cut 4 from muslin

★ Add ¼-inch (6 mm) seam
allowance on all pieces.

★ Placement guides for facial
features are in gray. Do not cut
these face parts.

★ These pieces shown at full size
and do not need to be enlarged.

MERRY MERMAID

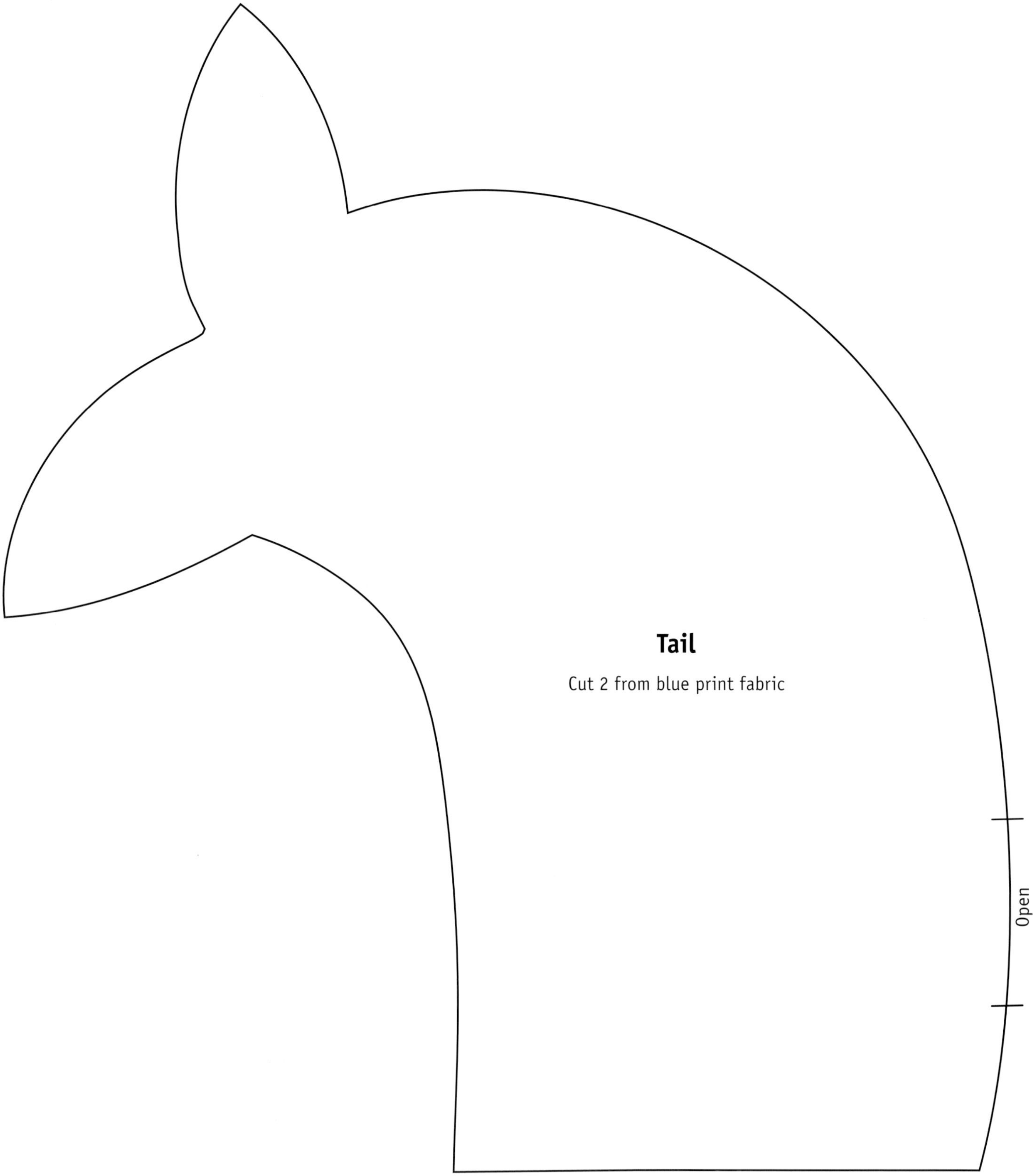

Tail

Cut 2 from blue print fabric

Open

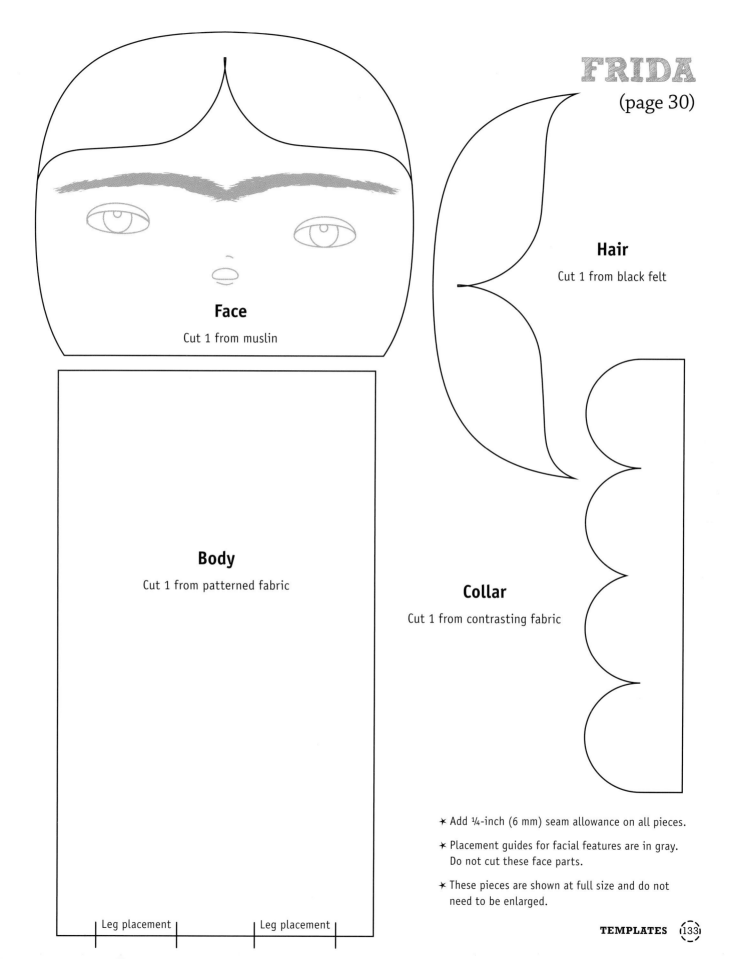

FRIDA
(page 30)

Face

Cut 1 from muslin

Hair

Cut 1 from black felt

Body

Cut 1 from patterned fabric

Collar

Cut 1 from contrasting fabric

Leg placement   Leg placement

★ Add ¼-inch (6 mm) seam allowance on all pieces.

★ Placement guides for facial features are in gray.
   Do not cut these face parts.

★ These pieces are shown at full size and do not
   need to be enlarged.

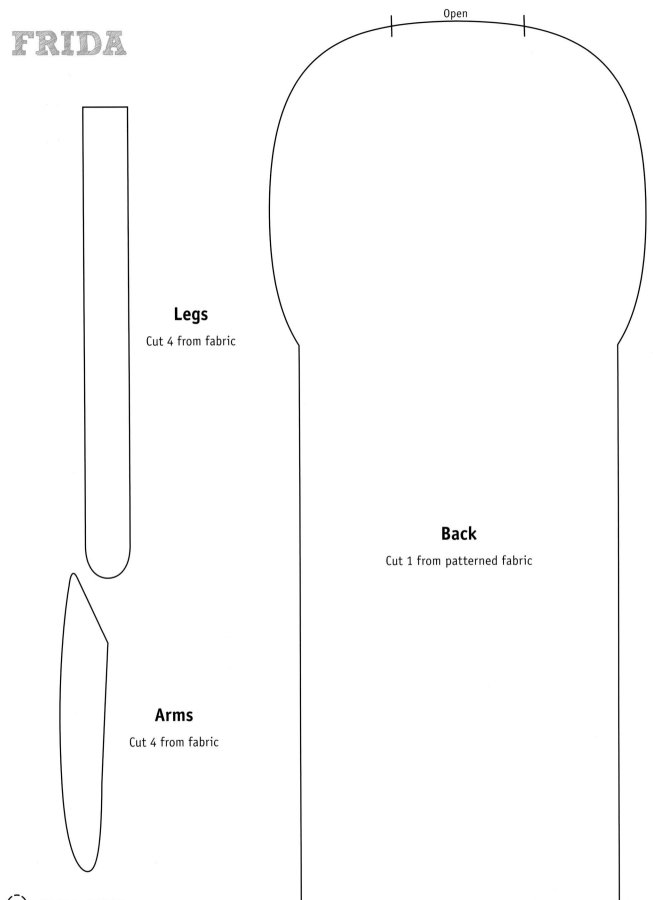

FRIDA

Legs

Cut 4 from fabric

Arms

Cut 4 from fabric

Open

Back

Cut 1 from patterned fabric

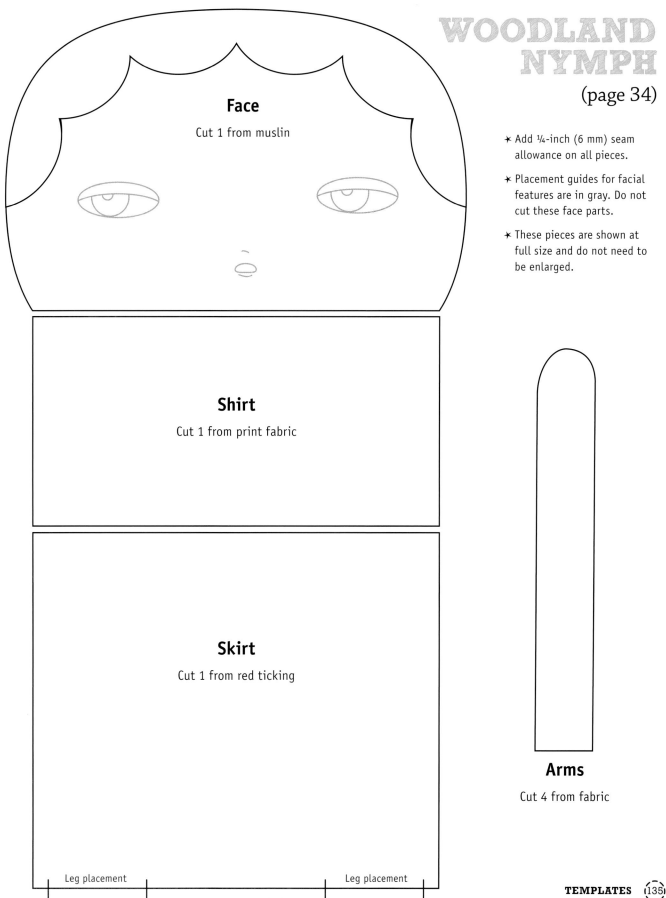

(page 34)

Face

Cut 1 from muslin

* Add ¼-inch (6 mm) seam allowance on all pieces.

* Placement guides for facial features are in gray. Do not cut these face parts.

* These pieces are shown at full size and do not need to be enlarged.

Shirt

Cut 1 from print fabric

Skirt

Cut 1 from red ticking

Arms

Cut 4 from fabric

Leg placement   Leg placement

WOODLAND NYMPH

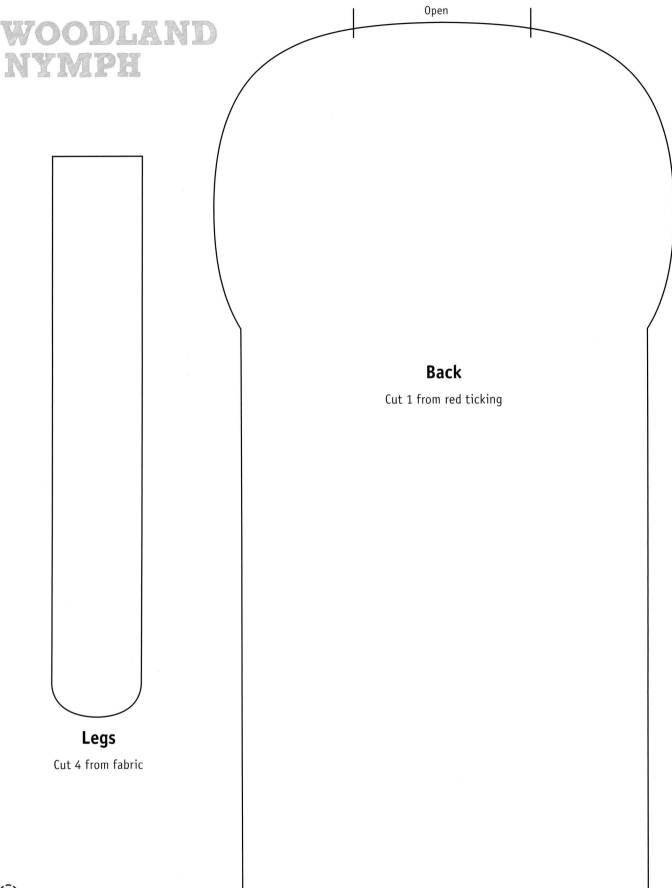

Open

Back

Cut 1 from red ticking

Legs

Cut 4 from fabric

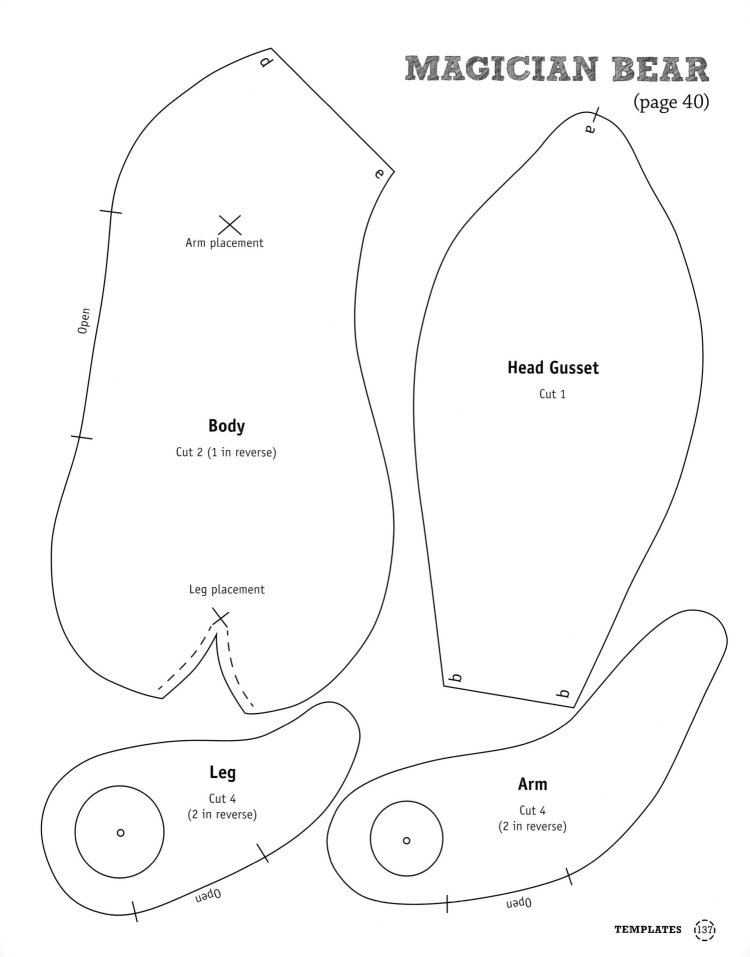

MAGICIAN BEAR

(page 40)

d

e

Arm placement

Open

Body

Cut 2 (1 in reverse)

Leg placement

a

Head Gusset

Cut 1

b

b

Leg

Cut 4
(2 in reverse)

Arm

Cut 4
(2 in reverse)

Open

Open

MAGICIAN BEAR

Head

Cut 2 (1 in reverse)

a

b   b

Vest Back

Cut 1

g   g

f   f

h   h

i   i

Neck

Cut 1

d

e

Ears

Cut 4

Vest Front

Cut 2 (1 in reverse)

i   h

f

f

LITTLE MISS MINI

(page 48)

★ These pieces are shown at full size and do not need to be enlarged.

Open

Ears

Trace 2 times on fabric per Before You Begin instructions on page 48

Body

Cut 2

Muzzle

Cut 1

Arms & Legs

Trace 4 times on fabric per Before You Begin instructions on page 48

Head

Cut 2

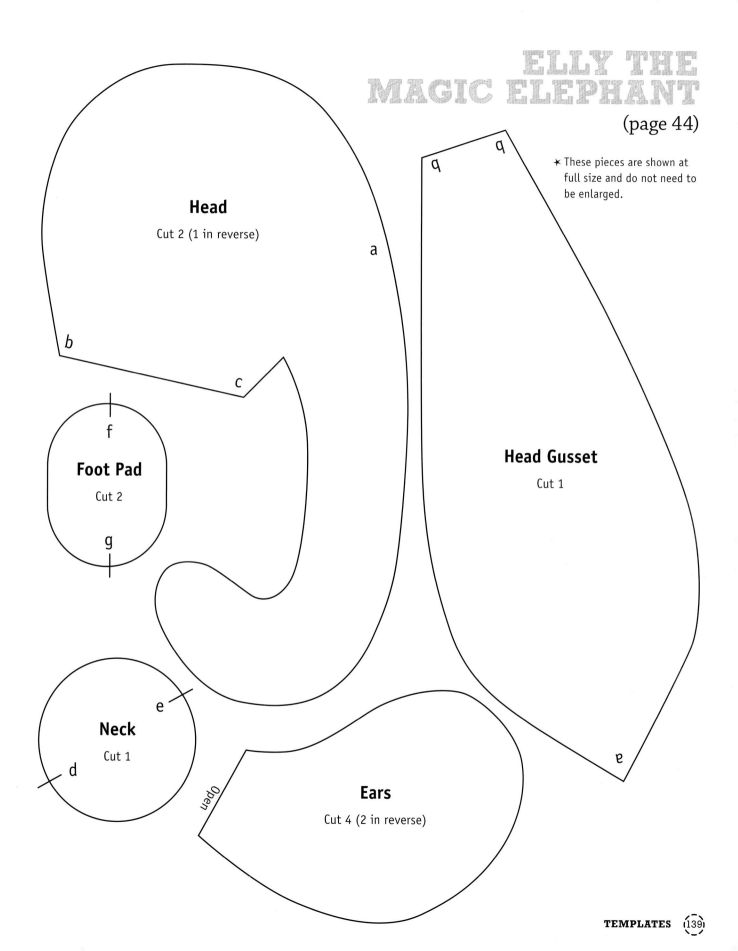

★ These pieces are shown at full size and do not need to be enlarged.

Head

Cut 2 (1 in reverse)

a

b

c

Foot Pad

Cut 2

f

g

Head Gusset

Cut 1

q

q

e

Neck

Cut 1

e

d

Open

Ears

Cut 4 (2 in reverse)

ELLY THE MAGIC ELEPHANT

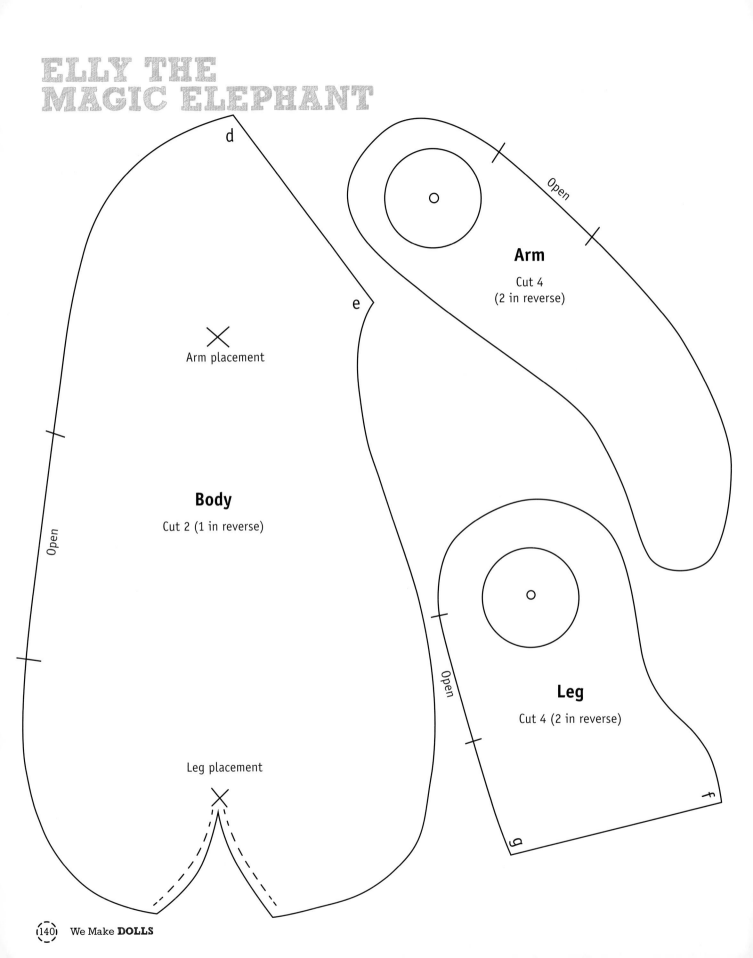

d

e

Arm placement

Body

Cut 2 (1 in reverse)

Open

Open

Leg placement

Arm

Cut 4
(2 in reverse)

Open

Leg

Cut 4 (2 in reverse)

Open

f

g

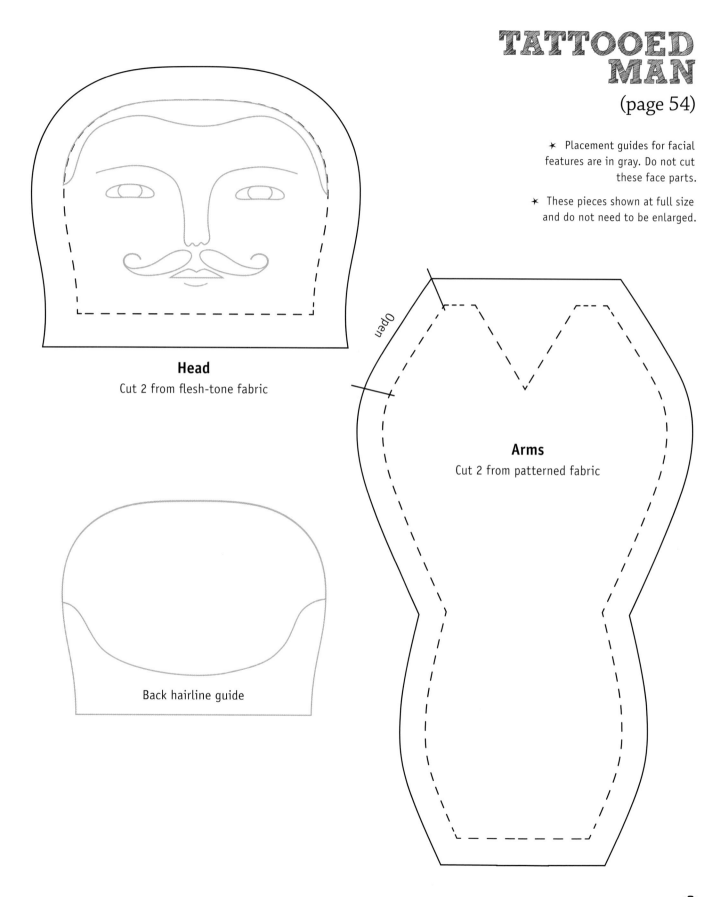

TATTOOED MAN

(page 54)

★ Placement guides for facial features are in gray. Do not cut these face parts.

★ These pieces shown at full size and do not need to be enlarged.

Head

Cut 2 from flesh-tone fabric

Back hairline guide

Open

Arms

Cut 2 from patterned fabric

TATTOOED MAN

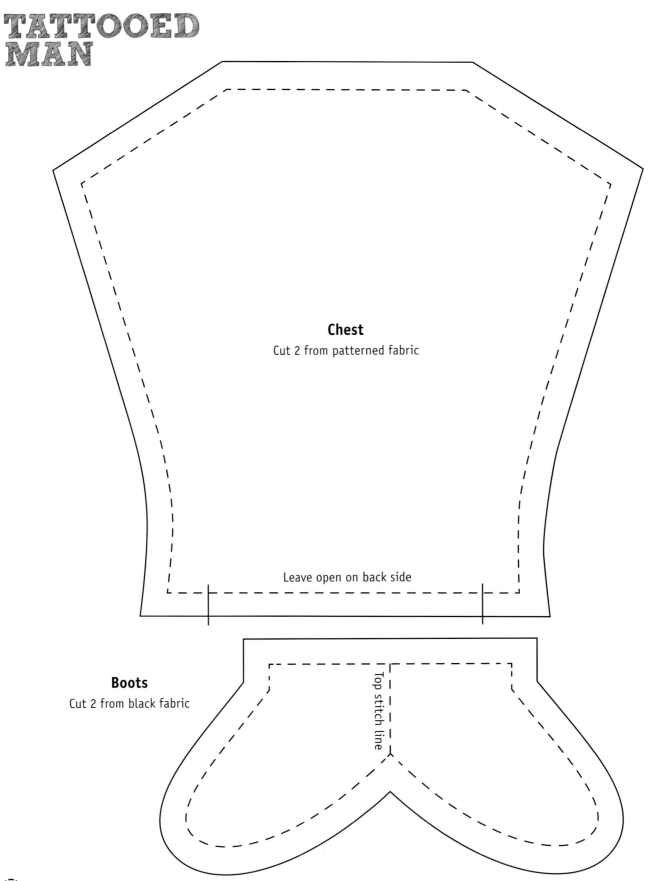

Chest

Cut 2 from patterned fabric

Leave open on back side

Boots

Cut 2 from black fabric

Top stitch line

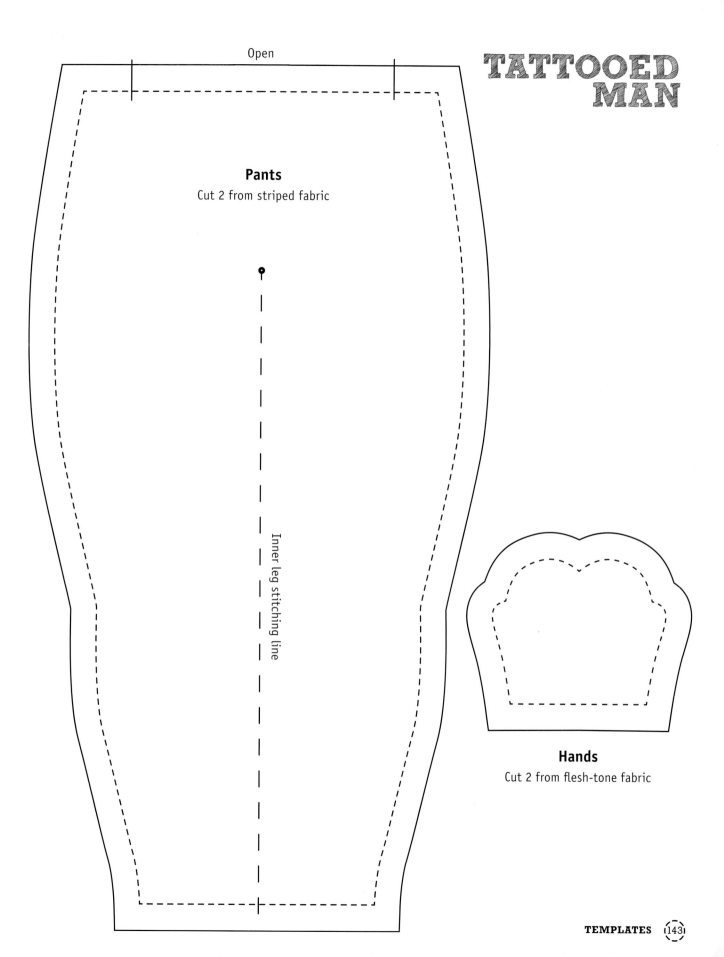

Open

TATTOOED MAN

Pants
Cut 2 from striped fabric

Inner leg stitching line

Hands
Cut 2 from flesh-tone fabric

SWEATER BABY

(page 58)

★ Placement guides for facial features are in gray. Do not cut these face parts.

★ These pieces shown at full size and do not need to be enlarged.

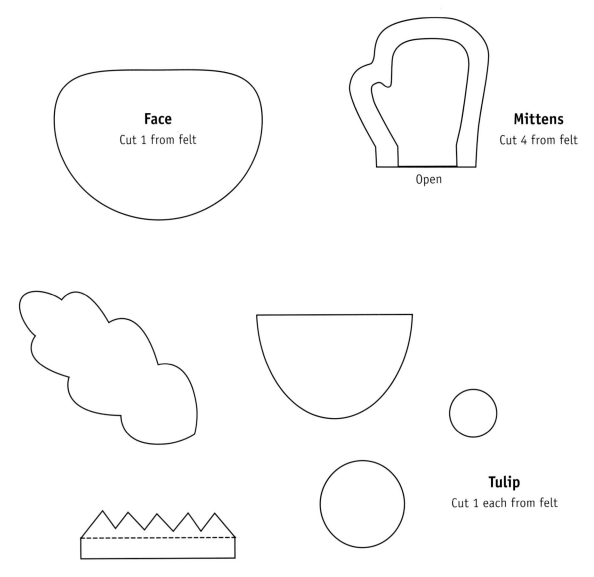

Face
Cut 1 from felt

Mittens
Cut 4 from felt

Open

Tulip
Cut 1 each from felt

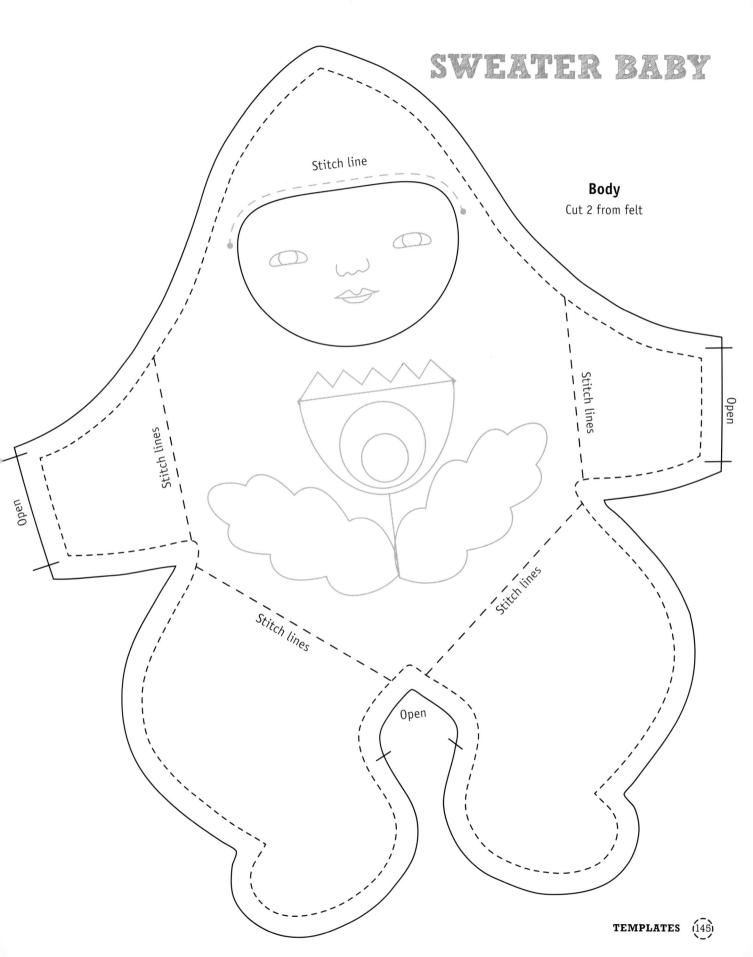

SWEATER BABY

Stitch line

Body
Cut 2 from felt

Stitch lines

Stitch lines

Open

Open

Stitch lines

Stitch lines

Open

JOSEFINA

(page 64)

★ Add a ¼-inch (6 mm)
  seam allowance to all pieces.

★ Placement guides for facial
  features are in gray. Do not cut
  these face parts.

★ These templates are shown at
  full size and do not need to be
  enlarged.

Open

Ear
placement

Bun
placement

Back Hair

Cut 1 from blue felt

Body

Cut 2 from
muslin

Cut 2 from
batting

Face

Cut 1 from muslin

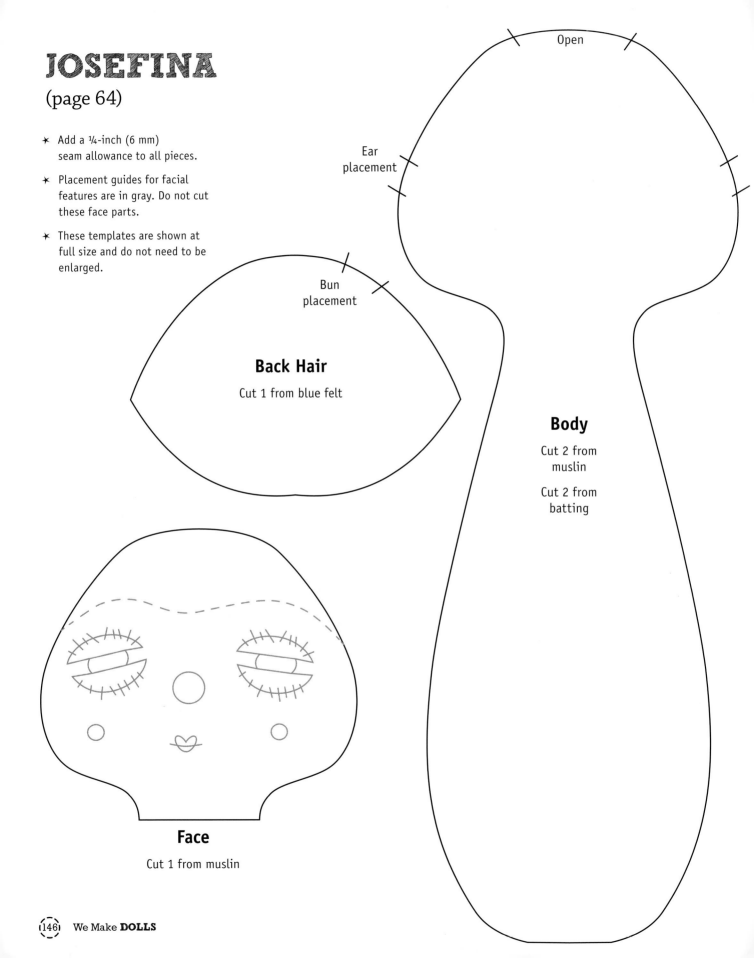

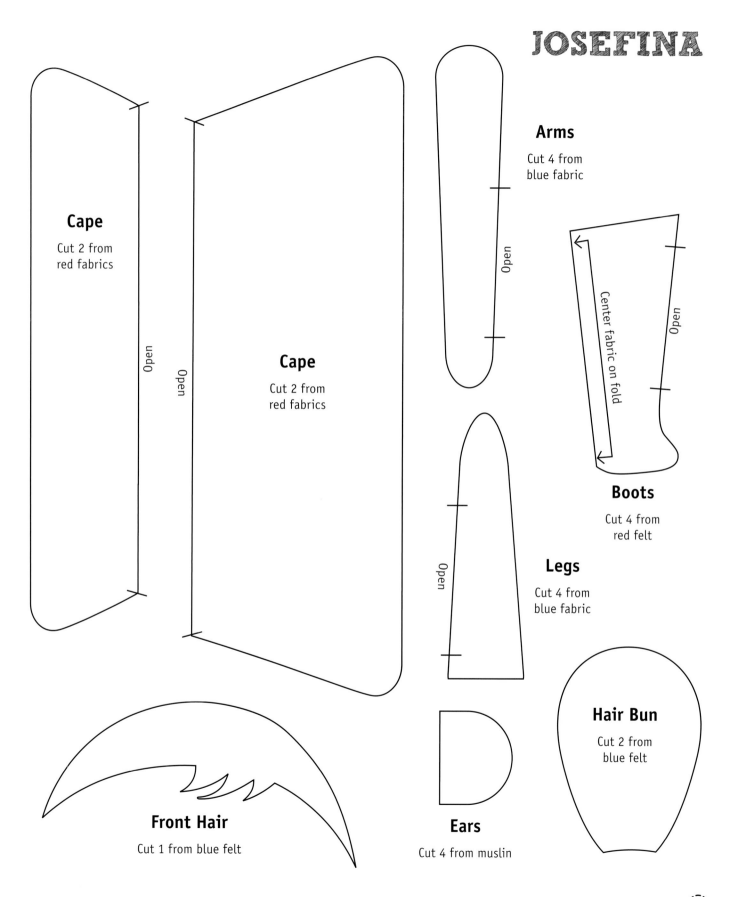

JOSEFINA

Arms

Cut 4 from
blue fabric

Open

Cape

Cut 2 from
red fabrics

Open

Open

Cape

Cut 2 from
red fabrics

Center fabric on fold

Open

Boots

Cut 4 from
red felt

Open

Legs

Cut 4 from
blue fabric

Hair Bun

Cut 2 from
blue felt

Front Hair

Cut 1 from blue felt

Ears

Cut 4 from muslin

BOBI DOG

(pg. 68)

★ Add a ¼-inch (6 mm) seam allowance to all pieces.

★ Placement guides for facial features in gray. Do not cut these face parts.

★ These templates are shown at full size and do not need to be enlarged.

Ear placement

Body

Cut 2 with wool suiting

Open

BOBI DOG

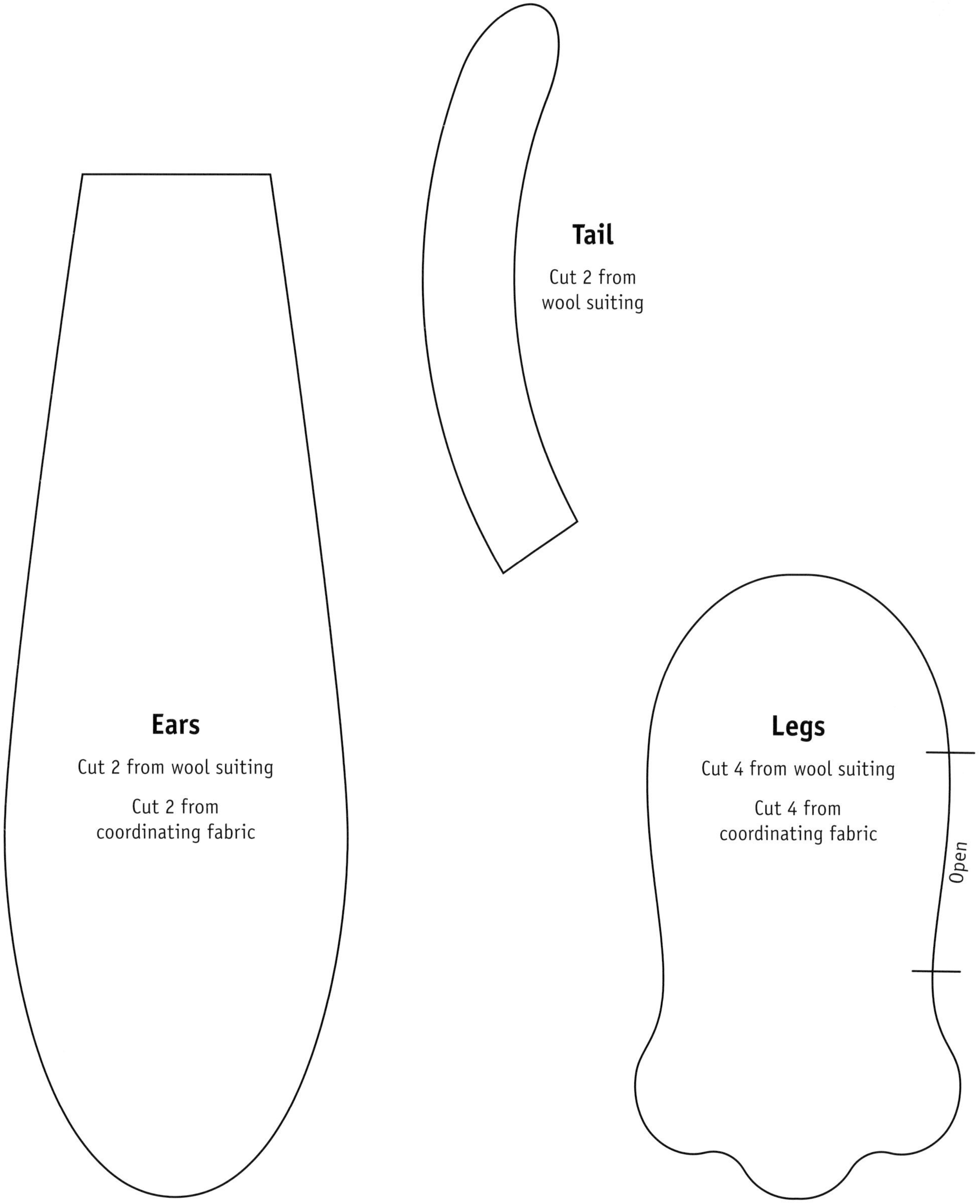

Tail

Cut 2 from
wool suiting

Ears

Cut 2 from wool suiting

Cut 2 from
coordinating fabric

Legs

Cut 4 from wool suiting

Cut 4 from
coordinating fabric

Open

ESTEFANIA

(page 74)

★ Add ¼-inch (6 mm) seam allowance on all pieces.

★ Placement guides for facial features are in gray. Do not cut these face parts.

★ These pieces are shown at full size and do not need to be enlarged.

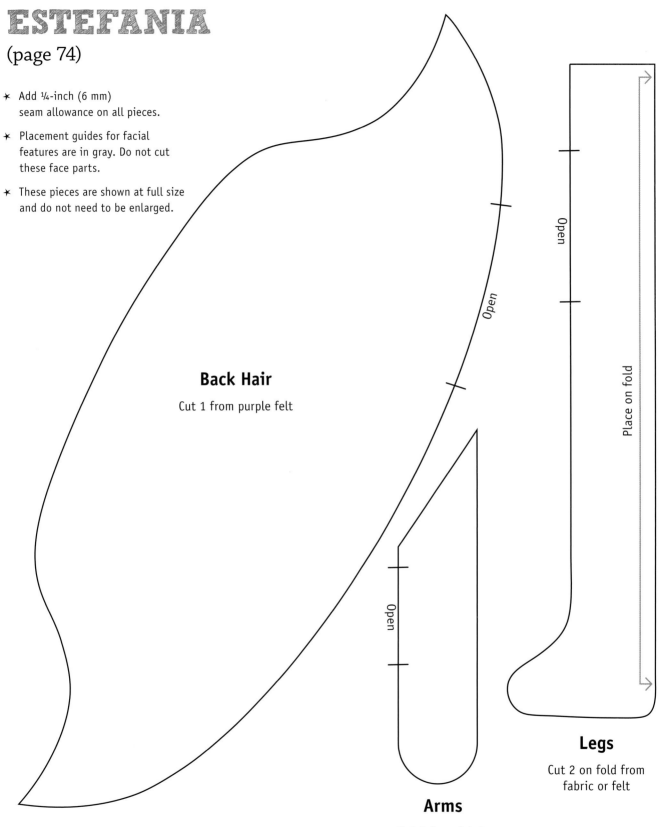

Back Hair

Cut 1 from purple felt

Open

Open

Place on fold

Arms

Cut 4 from fabric

Legs

Cut 2 on fold from fabric or felt

ESTEFANIA

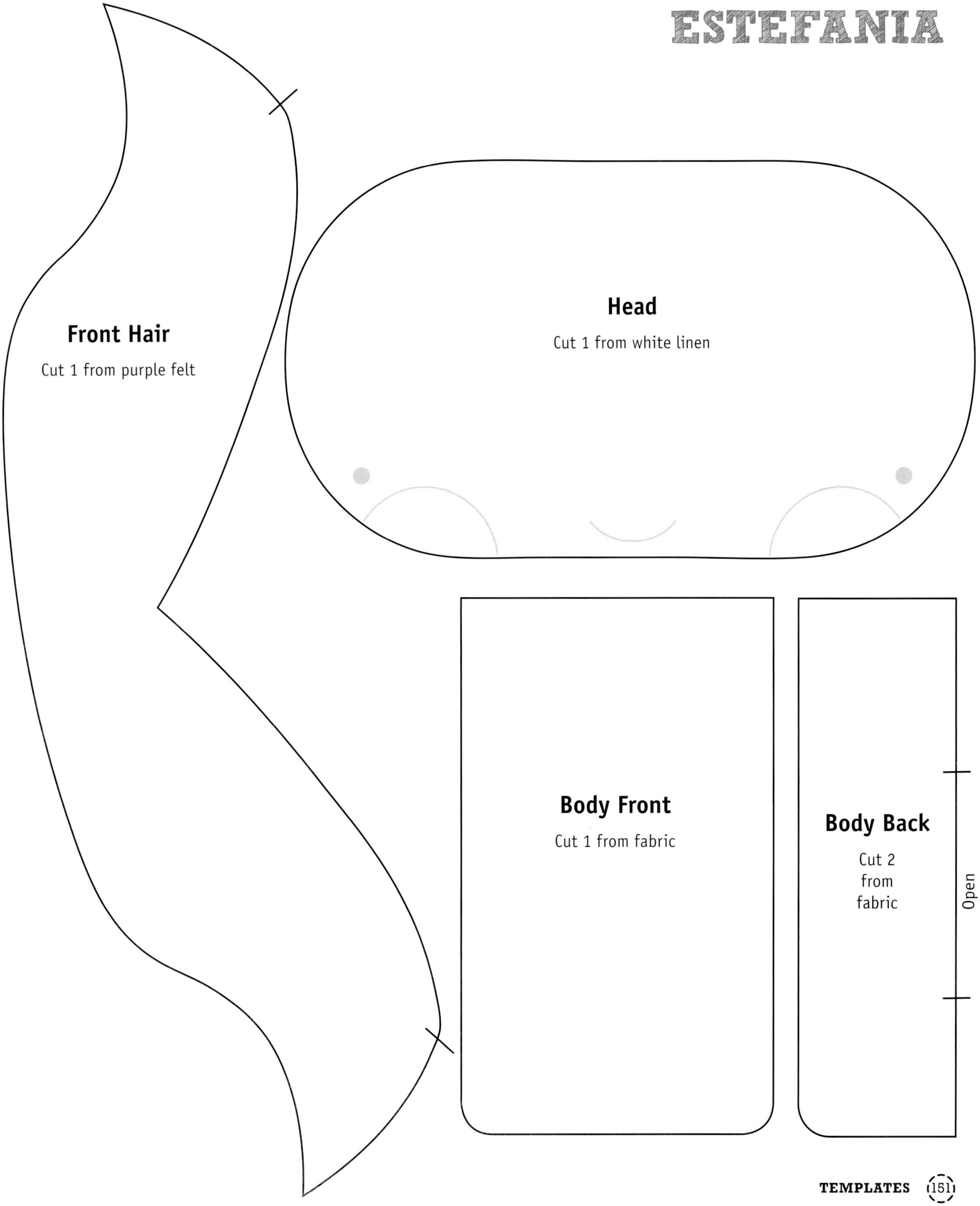

Front Hair

Cut 1 from purple felt

Head

Cut 1 from white linen

Body Front

Cut 1 from fabric

Body Back

Cut 2 from fabric

Open

FLEUR

(page 88)

★ Add a ¼-inch (6 mm) seam allowance to the body and head pieces only.

★ Placement guides for facial features are in gray. Do not cut these face parts.

★ Enlarge all template pieces for Fleur by 40 percent.

Body

Cut 2 from main fabric

Open

FLEUR

Head

Cut 1 from contrasting fabric

Hair

Cut 1 from brown felt

Face

Cut 1 from
flesh-tone felt

Cheeks

Cut 2 from felt

Bird

Cut 2 from fabric

Leaf

Cut 2
from felt

Color #2

Cut 2
from felt

Wing

Cut 2 from felt

fleur

Cut 1 from linen

Color #1

Cut 2
from felt

Color #1

Cut 2
from felt

Color #2

Cut 2
from felt

RED MATRYOSHKA

(page 92)

★ Add a ¼-inch (6 mm) seam
  allowance to the head and body
  pieces only.

★ Placement guides for facial
  features are in gray. Do not cut
  these face parts.

★ Enlarge all template pieces for
  Red Matryoshka by 40 percent.

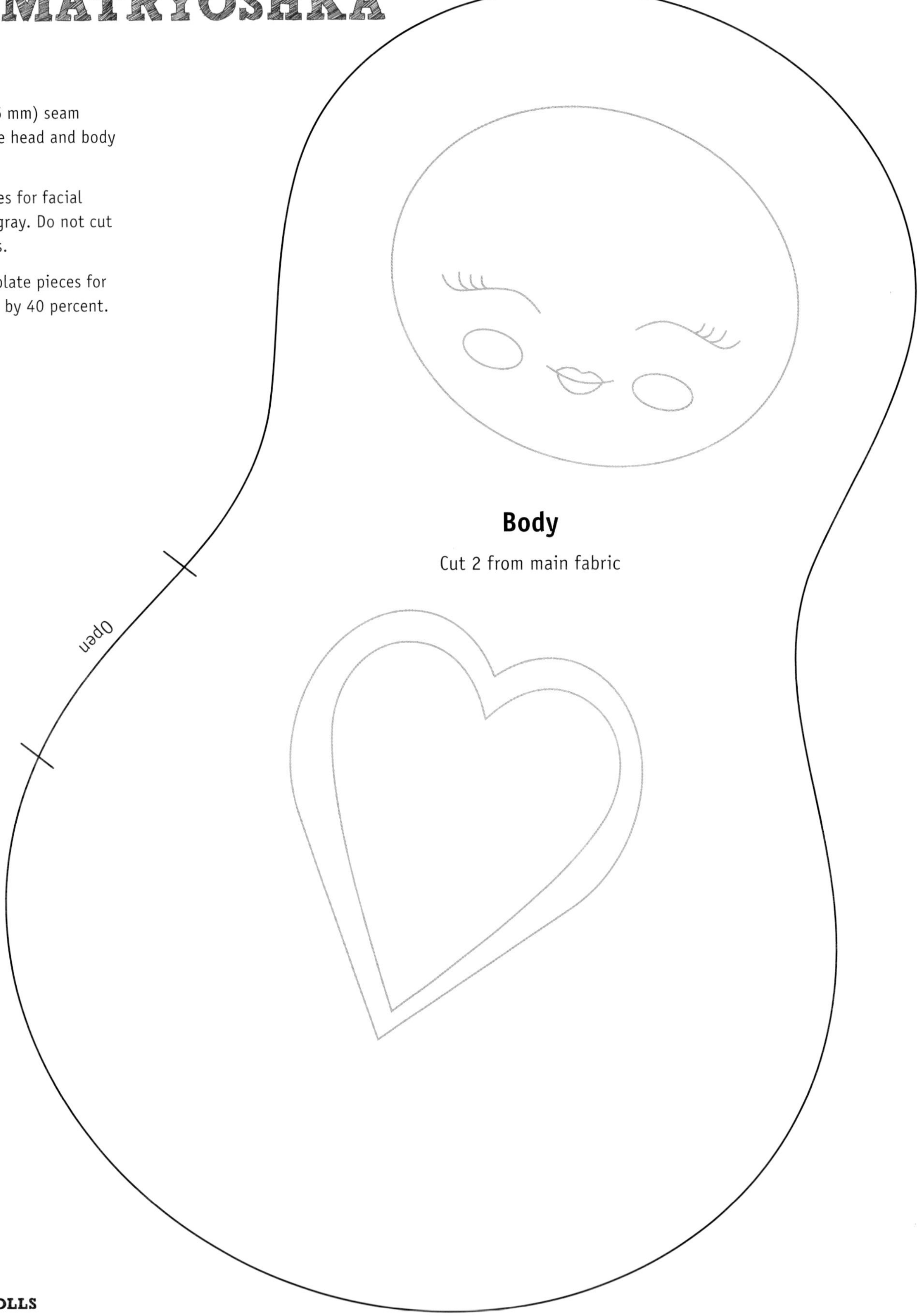

Open

Body

Cut 2 from main fabric

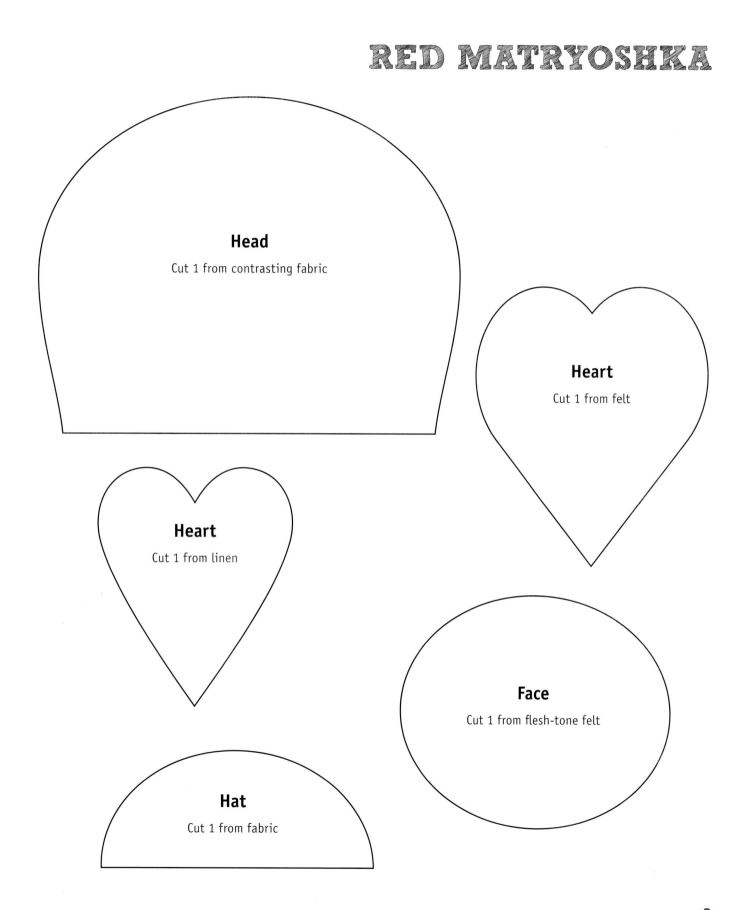

Head

Cut 1 from contrasting fabric

Heart

Cut 1 from felt

Heart

Cut 1 from linen

Face

Cut 1 from flesh-tone felt

Hat

Cut 1 from fabric

RED RIDING HOOD

(page 114)

★ Add ¼-inch (6 mm)
  seam allowance on all pieces.

★ Placement guides for facial
  features are in gray. Do not cut
  these face parts.

★ These pieces are shown
  at full size and do not
  need to be enlarged.

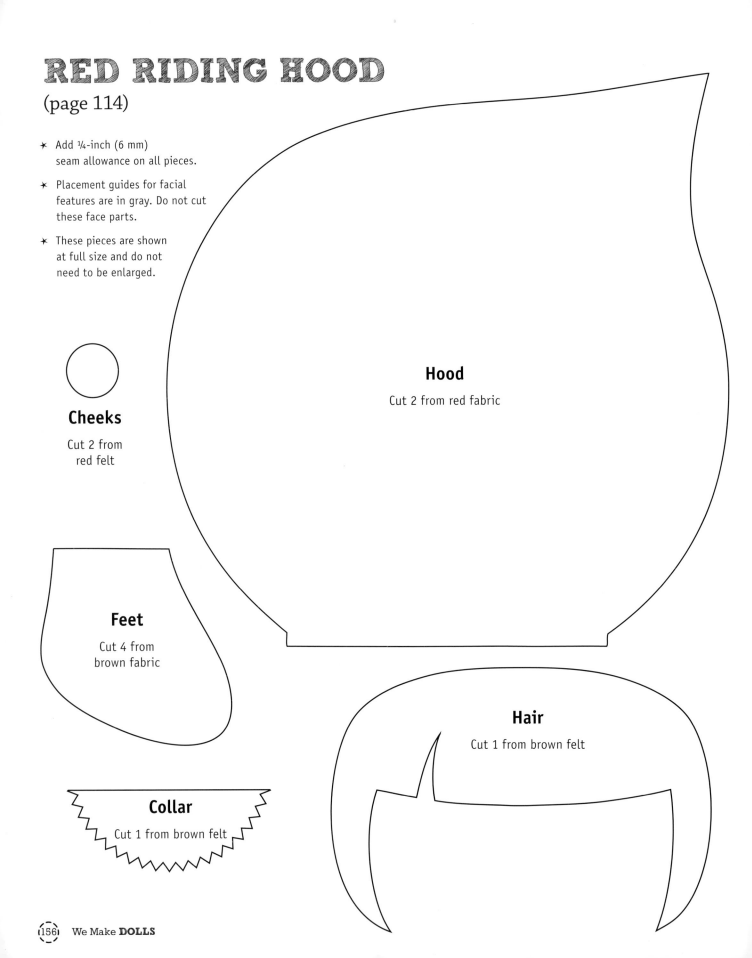

Cheeks

Cut 2 from
red felt

Hood

Cut 2 from red fabric

Feet

Cut 4 from
brown fabric

Hair

Cut 1 from brown felt

Collar

Cut 1 from brown felt

RED RIDING HOOD

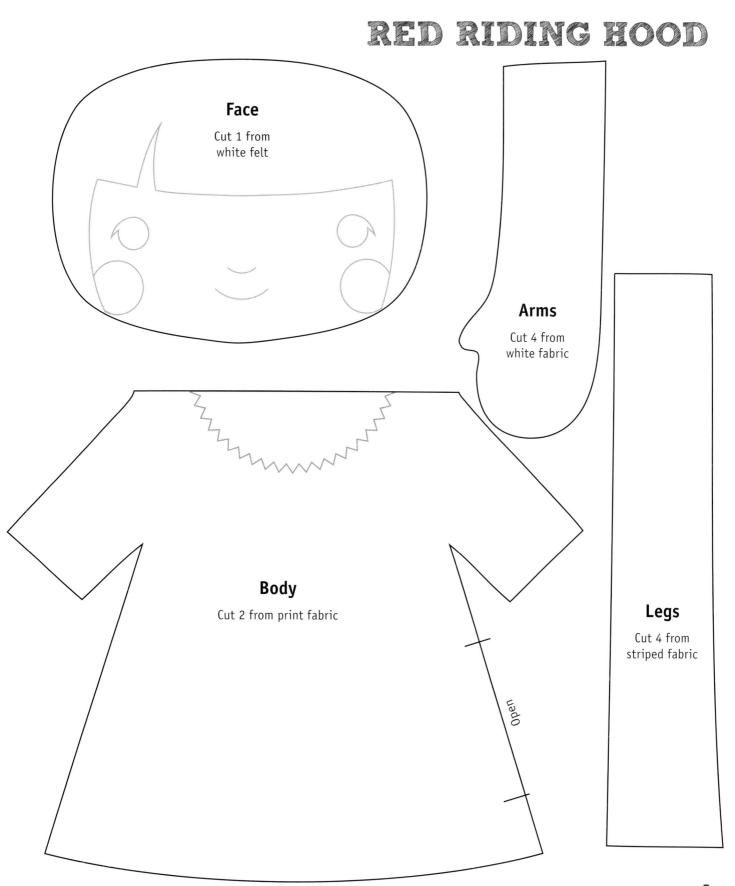

Face

Cut 1 from
white felt

Arms

Cut 4 from
white fabric

Body

Cut 2 from print fabric

Legs

Cut 4 from
striped fabric

Open

LOVELY LITTLE LAMB

(page 120)

★ These pieces shown at full size and do not need to be enlarged.

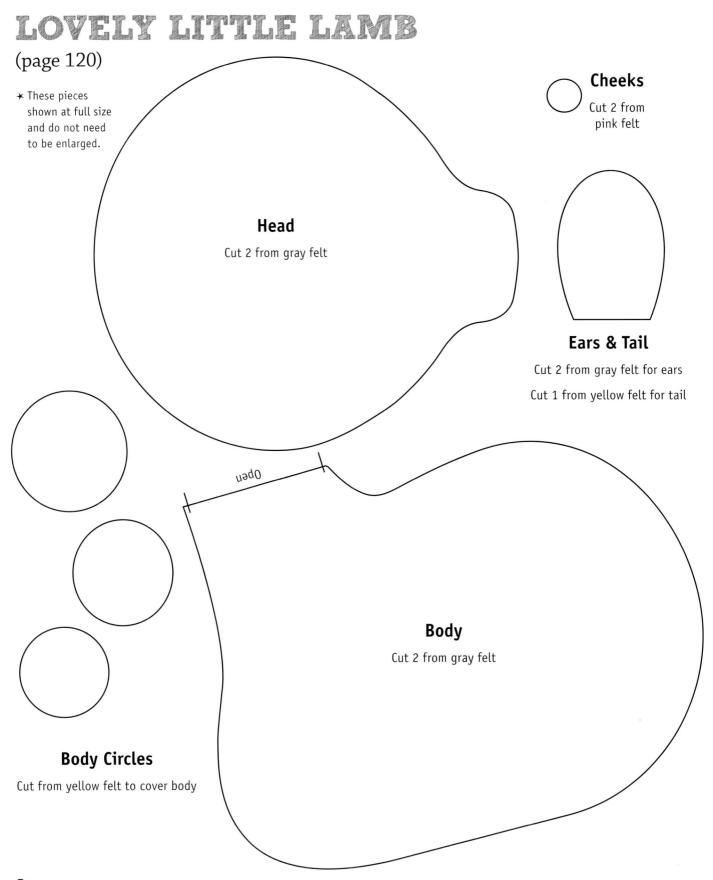

Cheeks
Cut 2 from pink felt

Head
Cut 2 from gray felt

Ears & Tail

Cut 2 from gray felt for ears

Cut 1 from yellow felt for tail

Open

Body
Cut 2 from gray felt

Body Circles

Cut from yellow felt to cover body

appliqué. A small layer of fabric attached to a larger base piece using either hand or machine stitching.

artificial sinew. Strong thread made of artificial fibers which has the feel and strength of natural sinew made from animal tendons. Dollmakers use artificial sinew to secure beads and sew through leather.

awl. A tool with a pointed spike set in a handle which is used to create holes in fabric, metal, paper, and wood.

batting. Flattened wadding made of cotton, polyester, or wool. Sold as a roll, it's most commonly used as the center layer when quilting.

crazy quilt. A quilt made by attaching irregularly shaped pieces of fabric onto a base fabric.

darning foot. A sewing-machine foot used when darning or for free motion sewing.

doll needle. Dollmakers use this long, sturdy, sharp needle for attaching doll parts. The length allows it to easily pass through the body of a soft doll. It comes in different lengths, but is typically 5 inches (12.7 cm) long.

embroidery floss. Dollmakers use embroidery floss to create facial features and other small details, including appliqué work. It is cotton thread with a slight sheen and loosely twisted individual strands.

fabric glue. An adhesive formulated for use on fabrics.

fat quarter. A piece of fabric that is one-fourth of a yard, cut to measure 18 x 22 inches (45.7 x 55.9 cm)

faux fur. Fabric made of synthetic fibers to resemble animal fur.

feed dogs. Metal bars in the throat plate of a sewing machine that grip and pull the fabric during the sewing process. Most sewing machines allow you to lower them so they won't grab the fabric when free motion sewing.

felt fabric. This is a non-woven material which you can purchase in precut sheets or off a bolt. Synthetic felt fabrics are less expensive but need to be used with caution since direct contact with heat may cause it to warp and melt. Wool or bamboo blends are more expensive but will not warp or melt like synthetic felt.

felting needle. A sharp, barbed needle used for needle felting. As you repeatedly poke tufts of roving, the barbs on the end of the needle make the fibers bond, which allow you to create firm shapes.

free motion sewing. A machine-stitching technique made by lowering the feed dogs on your machine which allows you to freely move the fabric.

fussy cut. A technique defined as cutting a specific motif from a printed fabric.

gusset. A piece of cut fabric inserted into a seam used to shape the garment or allow for movement.

hemostat. This surgical tool, which looks like scissors, is used by dollmakers to aid in stuffing.

joint disc. Used in conjunction with T-cotter pins, joint discs secure limbs to dolls while allowing the limbs to move.

mineral granules. Dollmakers use these granules when stuffing dolls to give the dolls weight. They are made of asphalt-based roofing substance.

muslin. A fabric made of loosely woven cotton.

needle felting. This is the technique of repeatedly poking tufts of wool roving with a sharp felting needle to create shapes and forms. By needle felting the shapes and forms together, you can sculpt a doll.

needle felting foam. This sturdy, thick, foam pad provides a guide for a felting needle when repeatedly poking the roving.

nylon beading cord. Nylon cord used specifically for attaching beads, frequently used to make knots in between.

perle cotton. This 2-ply cotton thread with high sheen comes in five different sizes and is used for embroidery and appliqué work.

pinking shears. The saw-toothed blades on these scissors are used for creating decorative edges and to prevent cut fabric edges from raveling.

polyester fiberfill. Dollmakers use this lightweight synthetic fiber for stuffing dolls.

roving. Wool fibers that have been combed and prepared before being spun into yarn. Dollmakers use it when needle felting. The sharp felting needle bonds the fibers of the roving, allowing the dollmaker to make firm shapes which, when attached to one another, become a sculpted doll.

seam allowance. This is the area between the edge of the fabric and the stitching line when stitching two pieces of fabric together.

spray fabric adhesive. Use this fast-drying, spray adhesive when you want to quickly fix layers of fabric together.

tacky glue. This white glue dries clear while retaining its flexibility.

T-cotter pins. Used in conjunction with joint discs, T-cotter pins have a T-head, much like a T-pin, with two ends you bend when securing it on the joint disc.

tuft. A small cluster made from strands of yarn, wool roving, or other fibers.

water-soluble fabric marker. Non-toxic marker with water-soluble ink used to make temporary marks on fabric. To completely erase the marks, use a cloth dampened with water to dab them away.

wet felting. The process of shaping tufts of wool roving with hot soapy water, causing the wool to bond and take shape. Also, it's the process of shrinking knit or woven wool fabric to create felt.

wood wool. A stuffing material made from wood shavings, also called excelsior. It is a traditional stuffing for teddy bears.

ABOUT THE AUTHOR

Jenny Doh is founder of *www.crescendoh.com* and former Editor-in-Chief of *Somerset Studio* magazine. In addition to authoring books, Jenny loves to knit, crochet, stay fit, and play the cello. She lives with her husband and children in Santa Ana, California.

ACKNOWLEDGMENTS

I thank Nichol Brinkman, Danita, Sasha Pokrass, Mimi Kirchner, Maria Madeira, Ana Fernandes, Denise Ferragamo, Jenn Docherty, Suse Bauer, and Katie Shelton for their tremendous doll designs. I thank Nicole McConville, Linda Kopp, and Kristi Pfeffer from Lark Crafts for their superb leadership and support. I thank Nadine Alvillar, B. Glass, Jane LaFerla, Gail Ellspermann, Cynthia Shaffer, Nancy D. Wood, and Jana Holstein for all of their hard work. I thank Gerardo, Monica, and Andrew for their love and support through thick and thin.

PHOTO CREDITS

Suse Bauer: Pages 6, 112–113

Sérgio Coutinho: Pages 62–63

Jenn Docherty: Pages 96–97

Jenny Doh: Pages 7, 42, 47, 51, 56, 66, 77, 80–81, 83–84, 103, 116

Denise Ferragamo: Pages 86–87

Ana Fernandes: Pages 72–73

Gonçalo Fernandes: Pages 72–73

Kerry Hawkins: Pages 52–53

Peter Hyde: Pages 52-53

Mimi Kirchner: Pages 52–53

Saül Martinez: Pages 24–25

Maria Madeira: Pages 62–63

Sasha Pockrass: Pages 38–39

Alexandra Rosier: Page 86

Jared Scarborough: Page 87

Cynthia Shaffer: Cover and pages 12, 14–16, 18–20, 22–23, 26, 28–30, 32–34, 36–37, 40, 42–43, 45–47, 49–51, 54, 56–57, 59–61, 65–68 70–71, 74–77, 79–81, 83–84, 89–92 94–95, 99–102, 104, 106–108, 111 114, 116, 121–122

Katie Shelton: Pages 118–119

Tall and Small Photography: Pages 10–11

Catarina Zimbarra: Pages 72–73

INDEX